GOSPEL F✝UNDATIONS

The Kingdom on Earth

| VOL. 6 | ACTS – REVELATION |

LifeWay Press® • Nashville, Tennessee

From the creators of *The Gospel Project*, Gospel Foundations is a six-volume resource that teaches the storyline of Scripture. It is comprehensive in scope yet concise enough to be completed in just one year. Each seven-session volume includes videos to help your group understand the way each text fits into the storyline of the Bible.

ISBN 978-1-5359-0363-9 • Item 005803637

Dewey decimal classification: 230
Subject headings: CHRISTIANITY / GOSPEL / SALVATION

EDITORIAL TEAM

Michael Kelley
Director, Groups Ministry

Brian Dembowczyk
Managing Editor

Joel Polk
Editorial Team Leader

Daniel Davis, Josh Hayes
Content Editors

Brian Daniel
Manager, Short-Term Discipleship

Darin Clark
Art Director

We believe that the Bible has God for its author; salvation for its end; and truth, without any mixture of error, for its matter and that all Scripture is totally true and trustworthy. To review LifeWay's doctrinal guideline, please visit lifeway.com/doctrinalguideline.

To order additional copies of this resource, write to LifeWay Resources Customer Service; One LifeWay Plaza; Nashville, TN 37234; fax 615-251-5933; call toll free 800-458-2772; or order online at LifeWay.com; email orderentry@lifeway.com.

Printed in the United States of America

Groups Ministry Publishing
LifeWay Resources
One LifeWay Plaza
Nashville, TN 37234

Contents

About *The Gospel Project*

Gospel Foundations is from the creators of *The Gospel Project*, which exists to point kids, students, and adults to the gospel of Jesus Christ through weekly group Bible studies and additional resources that show how God's plan of redemption unfolds throughout Scripture and still today, compelling them to join the mission of God.

The Gospel Project provides theological yet practical, age-appropriate Bible studies that immerse your entire church in the story of the gospel, helping to develop a gospel culture that leads to gospel mission.

Gospel Story

Immersing people of all ages in the storyline of Scripture: God's plan to rescue and redeem His creation through His Son, Jesus Christ.

Gospel Culture

Inspiring communities where the gospel saturates our experience and doubters become believers who become declarers of the gospel.

Gospel Mission

Empowering believers to live on mission, declaring the good news of the gospel in word and deed.

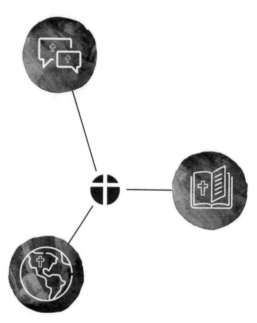

How to Use This Study

This Bible-study book includes seven weeks of content for group and personal study.

Group Study

Regardless of what day of the week your group meets, each week of content begins with the group session. Each group session uses the following format to facilitate simple yet meaningful interaction among group members and with God's Word.

Introducing the Study & Setting the Context
These pages include **content and questions** to get the conversation started and **infographics** to help group members see the flow of the biblical storyline.

Continuing the Discussion
Each session has a corresponding **teaching video** to help tell the Bible story. These videos have been created specifically to challenge the group to consider the entire story of the Bible. After watching the video, continue the **group discussion** by reading the Scripture passages and discussing the questions on these pages. Finally, conclude each group session with **a personal missional response** based on what God has said through His Word.

Personal Study

Three personal studies are provided for each session to take individuals deeper into Scripture and to supplement the content introduced in the group study. With **biblical teaching and introspective questions**, these sections challenge individuals to grow in their understanding of God's Word and to respond in faith.

Leader Guide

A tear-out leader guide for each session is provided on pages 95-108, which includes possible answers to questions highlighted with an icon and suggestions for various sections of the group study.

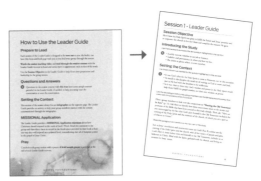

God's Word to You

The Good News That Awaits Us

"And they all lived happily ever after."

This is the coda, the postscript that punctuates the tales of our childhoods. The prince is victorious. The dragon is defeated. The princess is rescued. The struggle is over. The battle is won. And finally, "they all lived happily ever after."

The Bible has its coda as well. But unlike the happily-ever-afters of fairy tales, this is one of expectation—not for the end to come but for the next chapter to be written. A promise summarized in three words: "Come, Lord Jesus" (Rev. 22:20). This is the promise the entire story of Scripture builds toward. It is the deepest longing of the heart of God's people. The first man and woman longed for the coming of the Son, the One whose heel would crush the head of the serpent (Gen. 3:15). Abraham longed for the promised Offspring through whom all nations would be blessed (Gen. 12:3,7). David longed to see his Lord, the Son who would sit on the throne of an unfading kingdom (Ps. 110:1). God's people in exile and return longed for the coming of the Servant who would restore them (Isa. 49:6-7).

Then the long-expected One came—Jesus, the Son of David, the Son of Abraham, the Son of Eve, the Son of God—bringing redemption and peace with God by humbling Himself to the point of death and then being exalted in His resurrection (Phil. 2:8-11).

News of the reconciliation Jesus offered spread throughout the world. People of every tribe and tongue and nation believed and trusted Christ for the forgiveness of their sins. And as this good news continued to spread, the promise spread with it—the promise that tells of the day when Jesus returns to make all things new. When every tear will be wiped from every eye. When suffering, sadness, and death will be no more. In their place will be joy, gladness, and life everlasting as God dwells with His people forevermore.

But for now, we wait. And as we do, we join with our brothers and sisters across the centuries as we long for that day to come, echoing these words: "Amen! Come, Lord Jesus!"

The Spirit Comes

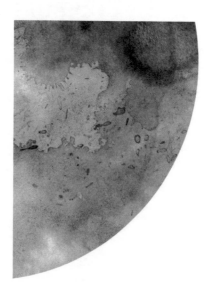

Introducing the Study

As the risen Savior and Lord, Jesus has all authority in heaven and on earth, so He has given His disciples their marching orders. The kingdom of God came in the person of Christ, and His disciples are to make it the mission of their lives to spread the good news of the gospel to every nation on earth. God told Abraham centuries ago that his descendants would bring blessing to the nations; that promise is fulfilled in Jesus and His disciples as active participants in God's global purpose of redemption.

 What are some of the competing priorities Jesus' commission forces us to rethink?

The task Jesus gave His disciples was massive. Impossible even. Which is why Jesus did not send His followers out alone. He promised that He would be with them always, even to the end of the age. God's enduring presence in the life of believers would come in the person of the Holy Spirit. The Spirit provides Christ's followers with the courage and conviction necessary to complete the mission of God.

What is the most challenging part of making Jesus' Great Commission the focus of your life?

Setting the Context

Jesus continued to instruct and encourage His disciples for forty days after His resurrection. Then, just before He ascended into heaven, **Jesus clarified the mission** He was giving them. The disciples were to be Jesus' witnesses; they were to tell others about who He is and what He has done to provide salvation to the world. And this mission would take them to the ends of the earth, to every nation, tongue, and tribe. But first, they were to wait in Jerusalem for the Father's promise.

 Why do you think the disciples needed to wait? Why didn't the Father and the Son send the Holy Spirit immediately?

So they waited together for ten days, united in prayer, until the day of **Pentecost**. Pentecost was one of the pilgrim festivals, so this meant that Jews had traveled from all over to be in Jerusalem, swelling the city's population. The celebration of Pentecost marked the end of the grain harvest as the people rejoiced and gave thanks to God for the harvest blessings by offering the first portion of the harvest. The festival concluded with a shared meal—a party—celebrating God's provision.

But this Pentecost celebration would be like none other. It was during this Pentecost that Jesus' disciples would experience the provision of **the Holy Spirit**. The Book of Acts tells of the wonderful works of the Holy Spirit through Jesus' disciples. **"Hearing the Old Testament in Acts"** (p. 11) shows how even these events were foretold by God.

Why do you think so many Christians are confused about the Holy Spirit?

✝ CHRIST Connection

Jesus had instructed His disciples to wait for the Holy Spirit because the Spirit would empower them to be His witnesses on earth. Just as Jesus had promised, the Holy Spirit came upon the disciples, filled them, and empowered them at Pentecost, resulting in three thousand new believers. God gives the Holy Spirit to those who trust in Jesus as Lord and Savior, and the Spirit changes us to be more like Jesus.

Hearing the
Old Testament *in* Acts

OLD TESTAMENT	NEW TESTAMENT
The Tower of Babylon God Confused Humanity with Different Languages (Gen. 11:1-9)	**Pentecost** The Filling with the Holy Spirit Overcame Language Barriers (Acts 2:1-13)
The Promise of the Spirit God Will Pour Out His Spirit on All Humanity (Joel 2:28-32)	**The Outpouring of the Spirit** The Promise of the Spirit Fulfilled (Acts 2:14-21)
Opposition to the Messiah The Nations Plot in Vain Against the Lord's Anointed (Ps. 2)	**Opposition to the Church** The Messiah's People Prayed for Boldness (Acts 4:23-31)
The LORD Called and Sent Prophets for His Name to His People and the Nations (Jer. 1; Ezek. 2)	**Jesus** Called Saul to Take His Name to Gentiles, Kings, and Israelites (Acts 9; 22; 26)
David's House The Nations That Bear God's Name Will Be Included (Amos 9:11-12)	**The Church** The Gentiles Who Are Called by Jesus' Name Are Included (Acts 15:14-19)

Continuing the Discussion

▶ Watch this session's video, and then continue the group discussion using the following guide.

How would you describe the person and work of the Holy Spirit to a non-Christian?

How do Christians experience the person and work of the Holy Spirit in their lives?

As a group, read Acts 2:1-4.

✳ How does this passage reveal both the power and the purpose of the Holy Spirit?

Why is it significant that the tongues of fire rested on each believer?

In the Old Testament, the Holy Spirit would come to a prophet temporarily for a specific purpose. But at Pentecost, the Holy Spirit came to take up permanent residence in believers. The tongues of fire resting on each person was evidence of the Spirit's individual filling. The Spirit empowered the disciples to give themselves to God's mission of declaring the gospel, proven by their new ability to speak in the languages of those gathered for the festival.

As a group, read Acts 2:22-24,36-40.

What are the essential components of sharing the gospel based on this section of Peter's sermon?

✳ Why is it important that Peter gave the people a way to respond?

In what ways might we overcomplicate the gospel as we share it?

Peter's sharing of the gospel convicted the crowd. When the Jews gathered around him heard about Jesus, they knew they needed to respond but didn't know how. Peter answered them and shared how they could be saved, and about three thousand people were added as believers that day. The newly-born church was growing.

As a group, read Acts 2:41-47.

What activities did the church engage in? Why was each vital?

✳ What does it mean that the early church was filled with awe of God? How might this relate to "the fear of the LORD"?

Do we have that same fear of God today? Why or why not?

Like the early church, the church today is to be devoted to the apostles' teaching, to fellowship, to breaking bread, and to prayer. These activities show how the church is built upon the Scriptures, gospel community, and spiritual development. As new believers joined the early church, we see that everyone was in awe, referring to a healthy fear and reverence of God. Accordingly, this fear arose as many signs and wonders, demonstrating God's hand on the church, were performed through the apostles.

✝ MISSIONAL Application

Record in this space at least one way you will apply the truth of Scripture as a believer indwelt by the Holy Spirit and empowered for the gospel mission.

Personal Study 1

The Holy Spirit comes to indwell every believer.

Read Acts 2:1-4.

During Jesus' final days on earth, before His crucifixion through His ascension, He promised the disciples that another Counselor—the Spirit—would come to carry on His work. He said, "If you love me, you will keep my commands. And I will ask the Father, and he will give you another Counselor to be with you forever. He is the Spirit of truth. The world is unable to receive him because it doesn't see him or know him. But you do know him, because he remains with you and will be in you" (John 14:15-17).

This is a wonderful Trinitarian statement—the Son asks the Father to send the Spirit. But before we get the wrong idea that these three Persons are somehow independent of one another, Jesus adds, "I will not leave you as orphans; I am coming to you" (John 14:18). As the Son and the Father are one, so are the Son and the Spirit. Although Jesus returned to the Father, the Counselor came and Jesus is still present.

Such is the mystery of the Trinity. God the Father, God the Son, and God the Holy Spirit are distinct yet one at the same time. We always need to hold these two truths together—God is one; God is Trinity. People have tried to illustrate the Trinity with examples like the forms of water or the parts of an egg, but these illustrations always fall short. We can't comprehend the Trinity. The doctrine is not illogical, but God's infinite being lies beyond human comprehension. The Trinity is not a riddle to solve through logic; it is a wonder to behold through faith.

When Jesus promised the Holy Spirit, He promised Himself too. He is seated at the right hand of the Father (Eph. 1:20; Heb. 8:1; 12:2) and He is also with us always, "to the end of the age" (Matt. 28:20). When the Holy Spirit is sent to us, God is present, and that, of course, means that Jesus Himself is present with us.

The disciples were bewildered by all that had happened leading up to and following Jesus' arrest and public execution. Days before the crucifixion, Jesus had arrived in Jerusalem like a king arriving for His coronation. The whole city greeted Him, hailing the new King of the Jews. Then He died on a cross. Something far *less* than they had expected had taken place. Rome remained in control of Jerusalem. There would be no new Israel—no freedom from the tyranny of their oppressors.

And yet, so much *more* than they had expected had taken place. Jesus had risen from the dead. They'd shared meals and conversations with Him. They'd touched His scars. They'd seen Him appear behind locked doors in a glorified body that was at once recognizable and unrecognizable, familiar and new. And they'd seen Him taken up into the heavens with the promise that He would come again in the same way. But first, the Spirit would come as Jesus had promised.

The story didn't end with Jesus' resurrection and ascension; instead, a new chapter began, one in which the Holy Spirit would fill every believer.

In the coming of the Spirit, Jesus' promise to be with us always was realized, as was the prophet Joel's promise that God would one day pour out His Spirit on "all humanity" (Joel 2:28). Likewise, the coming of the Spirit revealed the role that Christ's followers play in the world—not merely as a faithful group that remembers what Jesus has done, but as God's agents for good in the world and the very vessels God will use to carry out His mission. The advance of God's kingdom and the continuation of God's work through His church in His world would come through the Holy Spirit.

What questions or thoughts do you have about the filling of the Holy Spirit?

How should the indwelling of the Holy Spirit change the way we live?

Personal Study 2

The Holy Spirit comes to empower the spread of the gospel.

Read Acts 2:22-24,36-40.

It didn't take long after the Holy Spirit's arrival for Him to reveal the difference He would make to the church. When the Spirit arrived, He came with the sound of rushing wind. This sound caught the attention of the Jews gathered in Jerusalem from the nations for the festival of Pentecost. The Jews gathered to investigate and the disciples shared the good news of Jesus with them—in the language of each one gathered as the Spirit enabled them. Responding to the people's confusion, the apostle Peter, filled with the Spirit, stood before the massive crowd and preached the sermon recorded in Acts 2:22-40.

Peter couldn't contain himself. He nearly exploded as he shared this sermon, urgently pointing to Jesus as the Messiah, the One who came to liberate Israel from the oppressive burdens of sin and death. "Jesus is Lord and Messiah," Peter told the Jews, "and He rose from the dead and now sits at the right hand of the Father." But Peter wasn't the one talking that day; it was Peter *filled with the Spirit* who spoke. At the Spirit's urging, the words flowed from Peter's lips. He wove together the story of Jesus with passages from the Old Testament Scriptures and laid out the gospel for all to see.

This sermon provides a window into the life and nature of the Trinity. It was not merely Peter's love for the gospel that was on display, but the Spirit's love for the gospel and the Spirit's love for the Son as well. Each Person of the Trinity is enamored with the others. At Jesus' baptism, the Father said, "This is my beloved Son, with whom I am well-pleased" (Matt. 3:17).

Jesus, as we've already noted, talked glowingly about the coming of the Spirit and the good that would come with Him. And here, a Spirit-filled Peter preaches rapturously about what Jesus has accomplished and how the Father has honored Him, seating the resurrected Christ at His right hand. When John the apostle tells us that God is love, we don't have to look any further than the relationships within the Trinity to see that love displayed.

What we learn by looking at the Book of Acts is that the Spirit compels us to speak out as well. The mission of the church—to go out into the world and share the good news of God's reconciling work in Jesus—is a reflection of the heart of the Holy Spirit, who is more eager than anyone to celebrate the work of the Father and the Son.

We should understand that the immense power of the Holy Spirit is given to us as Christians specifically for the mission God has given us. The Holy Spirit is not like the electric company. The electric company provides a source of power, but its responsibility ends there. What appliances we plug in, how many lights we turn on and off, or how many extension cords we run is up to us. The electric company is neutral when it comes to the usage of the power it provides. The Holy Spirit, though, not only provides us with the power we need to live out God's mission, He directs us to give ourselves to that mission.

Knowing this should dramatically shift the way we think about sharing the gospel. You might find yourself struggling to speak up at times, to know when to share your faith, or to initiate conversations about Jesus. Some suggest techniques for making these conversations easier; many churches offer classes on the subject. And that's not a bad thing. But the easiest, and greatest, way to be bolder in sharing the gospel is by seeking to be filled with the Spirit (see Eph. 5:18-19; cf. Acts 13:50-52).

What prevents Christians from sharing the gospel with others?

How does the filling of the Holy Spirit overcome our barriers to share the gospel and empower our evangelism?

Personal Study 3

The Holy Spirit comes to build the community of faith.

Read Acts 2:41-47.

When the Holy Spirit comes to a new believer, He brings life and growth. This growth resembles that of a tree with its branches and roots. On one hand, the kingdom spreads into the world in visible, extensive ways characteristic of the church's mission. The momentum of this growth is overflowing and outward. But the kingdom also grows in ways often unseen with an inward momentum resulting in depth, stability, and holy relationships. We encounter this inward growth in Acts 2.

This passage records many demonstrations of God's grace and work. There are signs and wonders—miracles such as healing the sick and casting out demons—that characterized Jesus' ministry and the ministry of the apostles. But there are more subtle demonstrations as well. The believers shared their possessions, they sold what they had in abundance to help those in need among them. And they met regularly and shared meals.

This depth of community doesn't just happen. Most of the time, when you force people to live in tight, communal circumstances, the opposite occurs. Proximity leads to conflicts, and conflicts lead to strengthened borders. "Good fences make good neighbors," as they say. That's because there's less potential for conflict when what's mine is mine and what's yours is yours, and we both know which is which.

In Acts 2, however, this newly formed community presses into one another's lives, and the boundaries around possessions and wealth disappear. Moved by the Spirit, each believer's interests shifted from self to the good of the community of faith, and they began sharing all they had. They were sharing meals, sharing space, and sharing life.

What's more, as the church grew through the Book of Acts it came to include people of all different kinds of backgrounds. Because of the work of the Holy Spirit, people who were previously divided by race, economic status, or educational level were not only associating with one another, but actually *loving* one another. This type of love and unity is a powerful testimony. Not to the human spirit, because it is in our nature to divide into groups of people who look, think, and act like us. Instead, this unity testifies to the power of Christ through the Holy Spirit who breaks down the walls that keep us separated.

When the Holy Spirit takes up residence in our hearts, we begin to overflow with love for God and love for our neighbors, especially those who share our faith. These twin loves fuel the whole of the Christian life. It is love of God that leads us to bear witness to the gospel around the world, and it is love of our brothers and sisters that leads us to develop rich, deeply committed relationships with God's people.

Too often we emphasize one love over the other. When we focus only on the community of faith, we can lose touch with the wonder of God—sharing the gospel keeps that wonder fresh and alive in our hearts. Likewise, when we focus only on bearing witness to Jesus without developing any real relationships with other Christians, we find ourselves without accountability and often lacking the humility and gentleness that come as a result of being deeply known and deeply loved by the people around us.

What's displayed in Acts 2 comes as a result of the gift of God's Spirit. It cannot be controlled or manipulated or manufactured. It only comes when open hearts, stirred to faith by the gospel, receive this gift from the Father and the Son and are filled by Him. And so we seek this Spirit-transformed life not by imitating these behaviors but by seeking God's presence, by asking Him to fill us with His Spirit and renew our love for Him, His Word, His gospel, and His people.

How have you experienced deep community of faith in the name of Jesus and through the indwelling of the Holy Spirit?

What are some ways we can contribute to this Spirit-filled community of faith?

The Church
Is Scattered

Introducing the Study

God had kept His word once again—the Holy Spirit had come to the believers at Pentecost. And He still remains, indwelling every believer and empowering them to grow in Christ and give themselves to the mission of God. Through the Spirit, God also birthed the church, the body of Christ, which is unified not by race, economic status, or national origin but instead through the blood of Jesus. The early church began in Jerusalem, but the community of faith continued to grow.

 What characterized this first Christian community, and should characterize all Christian churches?

The church was growing, but it was not yet expanding. The church was meant to spread out, to be Christ's witnesses fanning out in mission across the globe. Soon the church would begin this outward movement because of a surprising reason: persecution. God would make the gospel known far and wide through suffering.

What do you think was challenging for the early church?

Setting the Context

The church was born in an extraordinary way, accompanied by the amazing signs of the Holy Spirit's arrival, a bold sermon, and thousands trusting in Christ, with more believers added to the church every day. The church in Jerusalem was living together in fellowship and growing in their faith. But this nearly ideal beginning would not last.

Before long, **Peter and John** healed a man who was lame and proclaimed the gospel, claiming that the healing was evidence of Jesus' resurrection and calling people to repent and believe. This was too much for the same religious aristocracy who had orchestrated the crucifixion of Jesus just weeks before. Peter and John were arrested and forbidden from speaking in the name of Jesus—the first act of persecution against the church that would soon escalate toward violence. **"Suffering for Jesus"** (p. 23) traces this progression of persecution against the church.

 What is it about suffering that can make it such a powerful testimony to Christ?

Despite the threats of the officials, Peter and John and the rest of the church continued to proclaim the gospel. Telling others about Jesus was the central mission of the church, and they could not stop. **Stephen**, one of the first deacons, or servants, in the church, spoke the gospel with courage and faith, and he would be the spark God used that ignited widespread persecution and the scattering of the church from Jerusalem.

> How have you seen or heard of God using suffering to advance the gospel?

✝ CHRIST Connection

In his death as the first Christian martyr, Stephen followed in the footsteps of His Savior. Both Jesus and Stephen were falsely accused and charged for blasphemy. Both Jesus and Stephen prayed for their executioners. Both Jesus and Stephen entrusted their spirits to God as they died. As a follower of Jesus Christ, Stephen reflected his Master in life and in death and will again at the resurrection.

Suffering *for Jesus*

Acts of MINISTRY	The Form of PERSECUTION	The RESULTS
Peter, along with John, healed a lame man and then preached in Jesus' name (Acts 3:1-26)	• Peter and John were arrested by the Sanhedrin and threatened if they spoke in Jesus' name again (Acts 4:3-22)	• The church prayed for boldness in the face of opposition, which the Lord granted through His Holy Spirit (Acts 4:23-31)
Through the apostles, the sick and those with unclean spirits were being healed (Acts 5:12-16)	• The apostles were arrested and tried by the Sanhedrin, flogged and ordered not to speak in Jesus' name (Acts 5:18-41)	• The apostles rejoiced that they were counted worthy to suffer for Jesus' name and continued proclaiming the good news about Jesus (Acts 5:41-42)
Stephen performed great wonders and signs among the people and spoke with wisdom from the Holy Spirit (Acts 6:8-10; 7:1-53)	• Stephen was falsely accused of blasphemy against the temple and taken outside the city and stoned to death (Acts 6:11-14; 7:57-60)	• Stephen prayed for forgiveness for those stoning him (Acts 7:59-60) • Persecution broke out against the church and scattered believers throughout the world preaching the word about Jesus (Acts 8:1,4; 11:19-20)

Continuing the Discussion

Watch this session's video, and then continue the group discussion using the following guide.

How does the story of Stephen reveal God's ability to bring good results out of evil intentions?

What are some of the things we learn about faith under pressure from the account of Stephen?

As a group, read Acts 6:8-10.

What attributes of Stephen are evident from these verses?

What are some of the ways we can and should rely on the Spirit as we tell others about the gospel?

Through God's favor and power, Stephen performed great wonders and signs among the people that supported the gospel he proclaimed. But some members of the Freedman's Synagogue opposed Stephen, and when they were unable to best him in a debate, they induced men to make false accusations against him. With charges in hand, the group took Stephen to the Sanhedrin, the Jews' high court.

As a group, read Acts 7:44-51.

What are some of the Old Testament stories that Stephen chose to reference in his defense against the Sanhedrin?

What does Stephen's use of Scripture reveal about how he viewed it?

How should Stephen's charge against the Sanhedrin shape the way we share the gospel?

Stephen's defense should have sounded familiar to the Jewish leaders—it came straight from the stories of their heritage in the Old Testament. Over and over again, their ancestors had rebelled against their loving God. And this generation had done the same with Jesus. That was the point Stephen was driving toward: They had treated Jesus in the same way as their ancestors had treated the Old Testament prophets. But the leaders missed the point, or chose to close their ears, minds, and hearts to it.

As a group, read Acts 7:54-60.

Why did the leaders react so violently against Stephen?

✱ What was the purpose of Stephen's vision of Jesus standing next to God's throne?

The Sanhedrin was enraged by Stephen's sermon, especially by his charge that they had received but not kept the law. There was nothing else to hear, so they led Stephen out to have him stoned. Stephen had preached Jesus; now it was time to show Jesus. Like Jesus, the Lamb of God who was led to the slaughter without resistance, Stephen knelt in an attitude of prayer and worship as angry men began hurling stones at him. Stephen was humble and faithful to the message of the gospel in word and deed, and God was honored. So much so that Stephen's vision of Jesus is of Him standing rather than sitting. Stephen died with a vision of His exalted Lord in his mind and immediately stepped into His presence. In the end, Stephen not only testified about the centrality of the gospel, he also lived that truth.

✝ MISSIONAL Application

Record in this space at least one way you will apply the truth of Scripture as a witness to the truth, grace, and glory of Jesus.

Personal Study 1

God's people speak boldly in the Spirit's power.

Read Acts 6:8-10.

Acts 6–7 records Stephen being persecuted for his testimony about Jesus. This is one of the earliest and most powerful stories of a Christian staring down suffering—even to the point of death.

Stephen was filled with the Holy Spirit and known for performing signs and wonders and testifying about Jesus. But success often breeds opposition. Not everyone received Stephen's message about Jesus and some argued with him, hoping to stop him from sharing the gospel. But God had given Stephen the Holy Spirit and wisdom so their efforts fell short.

This theme recurs throughout the Book of Acts: ordinary men like Stephen and Peter debate well-educated clergy and win. The Jewish leaders may have been stunned by these losses, but we should not be. Stephen and Peter had two unfair advantages from the start. First, they were on the side of the truth, which makes winning any debate much easier. And second, they were filled with the Holy Spirit, which gave them supernatural wisdom in what to say and when and how to say it.

Often, when we are confronted by unbelieving friends or an unbelieving culture, we look for an advantage in books or training. We want to learn how to defeat the world's arguments—how to tell others about Jesus in a way that cannot be refuted. There is value in this. We *should* study the story the world tells and how to tell the gospel story in a powerful way. Tools and techniques, however, are not ultimately what will make the difference. God's presence and the power of the Holy Spirit will. We would be better served in preparing for confrontation with the world through prayer, Bible reading, and worship.

Because the Jews could not defeat Stephen, they take him before the Sanhedrin, the body of religious leaders who oversaw the Jewish community. There, his opponents resort to low and dirty tactics, lying about what Stephen had been preaching and teaching.

We shouldn't be surprised if we experience something similar. As the culture around us becomes increasingly hostile to Christianity, we shouldn't be surprised if we find ourselves the objects of greater aggression.

And like the Jews in Stephen's day who could not refute the truth and had to lie to gain an advantage, those who oppose the gospel today will resort to the same tactic. Lying is one of Satan's preferred tactics, one those who would like to see Christianity disappear from the public sphere will put to good use.

In Acts 6–7, Stephen was accused of speaking blasphemy against the temple and against the law found in the Old Testament. We will most likely not be accused of such blasphemy, but we are likely to be charged with hateful speech, bias, and bigotry because of our convictions of the value of human life, the meaning of marriage, and the origins of sexuality. Even if we never utter a judgmental word, we might find ourselves accused. Here in Acts 6, we see that this is the nature of opposition to Christianity. It thrives on exaggeration, distortion, and lies in an attempt to discredit the work of the gospel.

Stephen did not pray for his own safety. Neither did he apologize for speaking out in the name of Jesus. Instead, he trusted that the Holy Spirit would continue to give him courage to live out God's mission of gospel demonstration. The same Spirit that empowered Stephen lives in us today and will, in our case, grant us the courage and wisdom to speak the good word of the gospel.

What role does the Holy Spirit play in our response to opposition?

What is our responsibility to prepare for the reality of opposition?

Personal Study 2

God's people proclaim God's Word with the Spirit's understanding.

Read Acts 7:44-51.

Eventually, Stephen is called on to speak. His response to the charges against him is recorded in Acts 7. Stephen's defense comes in the form of a stark rebuke with a clear testimony to Jesus as the fulfillment of the Old Testament, the very thing they've accused him of blaspheming.

Stephen's sermon might sound a bit odd to our ears. It's important to keep two things in mind when we read it so we understand how powerful its message is and why the reaction against it was so strong.

First, to Stephen's Jewish audience, there was nothing on earth as sacred as the temple. The temple in Jerusalem was the high point of Jewish history. As Jews, their exclusive claim was that the one true God dwelled with their people, first in the portable tabernacle and then in the permanent temple in Jerusalem. The temple was a vital symbol of God's presence and blessing and was an object of national pride.

Second, Israel was unfaithful to their covenant with God. Throughout their history, they turned to the gods and idols of their neighbors. Eventually, they were conquered, the temple was destroyed, and the nation was crushed. For generations, the temple was rubble. Its reconstruction came with a religious revival, and the second temple's presence in Jerusalem was seen as a sign that God would be coming back to Israel and they would one day be free from the tyranny of the nations.

When Stephen spoke about where God dwells, he and his audience had this history in mind. God had never been confined to these dwelling places, which no one in Israel disputed, but Stephen went further and told them that they were missing the point of what was happening in Israel right then. God had indeed come back to Israel, but He wasn't manifesting Himself in the temple; He was there in flesh and blood. The Righteous One had come, and they had killed Him.

By saying this, Stephen not only confronted them as those who killed Jesus, he also lumped them in with all those who had been unfaithful to God in Israel's history. Just as the unfaithful members of Israel had killed the prophets, their first-century sons had killed the One to whom the prophets had pointed.

They killed Jesus—God incarnate—and furthermore, now they were persecuting His church, where God the Holy Spirit lives in the hearts of Christ's people.

No doubt those listening to Stephen were shocked by what he said. It was shocking not only because of Stephen's charges against them, but also because Stephen had a different understanding of what the Old Testament stories meant. Like the travelers on the road to Emmaus in Luke 24, Stephen's eyes were opened to see that all the Law and the Prophets testify to Jesus Christ.

The same thing happens to us when we read God's Word. God's Spirit will open our eyes, our minds, and our hearts to understand and apply Scripture to our lives. The power of the Spirit is evident when we read the Bible and find it to be living, active, and sharper than a double edged sword, and yet someone else might read it and find it to be a dusty and stale manuscript. The Holy Spirit makes the difference.

When we proclaim God's Word, both to our own souls and to those around us, we can do so with confidence. But our confidence is not in our ability to speak articulately, argue convincingly, or illustrate eloquently. Instead, our confidence is in the power of the Holy Spirit who makes the Word of God come alive.

What posture of the mind and heart should we take as we read God's Word?

What are some ways you might express your faith in the power of God's Word in your daily habits?

Personal Study 3

God's people face persecution through the Spirit's filling.

Read Acts 7:54-60.

The response to Stephen was swift and terrible. Three details of this final scene in Stephen's life are worth noting because each shows us how the filling of the Holy Spirit affects the way we face opposition and persecution.

First, notice that God was with Stephen in the midst of this trial. When we hear stories of Christians enduring beatings, torture, and the threat of death while refusing to deny their faith, we often wonder how they did it. How were they able to sustain their faith under such pressure? It must have been tempting to deny their faith to save their lives. Wouldn't God understand? Wouldn't He forgive? And wouldn't it make sense to save their lives so they could continue preaching the gospel?

If Stephen felt that pressure, we don't have to wonder why he didn't cave. We're told why: Stephen was full of the Holy Spirit. As the intensity of persecution increased, so did God's sustaining provision—Stephen looked into heaven and saw God's glory with Jesus standing at God's right hand. Stephen couldn't deny Jesus' lordship in that moment because he saw it so clearly, perhaps more clearly than he ever had seen it before. So he cried out in joy and in worship, even as the mob raged against him.

We see a principle that reverberates throughout the Scriptures at work here: God will supply all we need to obey and follow Him. God provides what we need as we need it, and when suffering and trials come into our lives, we can be confident that God will supply the strength, support, and encouragement we need to remain faithful. God has never promised to deliver us from ordeals, but He has promised to carry us through them.

Second, we see that Stephen is right in his debate with the Jewish leaders, and he knows it, yet he does not become judgmental or arrogant. Yes, his rebuke to the leaders was harsh, but as Stephen dies, he cries out, "Lord, do not hold this sin against them!" Like Jesus, he cried out for God to be merciful to those who persecuted him (see Luke 23:34). His actions were motivated not by pride—an eagerness to be right and to prove his rightness—but by love. He wanted the Jews to see that he was right not merely to believe him, but so they would believe in Jesus. Preaching, evangelizing, and contending for the faith must come from a heart of love and compassion for the lost, not from an ego that wants to be proven right and to win.

Third, as the crowd gathered stones to kill Stephen, they piled their cloaks at the feet of a Jew named Saul. God would transform Saul's life—one of the church's most violent persecutors would become one of the church's most important church planters and theologians. Most of us know Saul as the apostle Paul. His presence at this moment reminds us that we never know what might result from our ministries and our words and that no one is beyond the grasp of God's grace.

Many people would point to Stephen's death and call it a failure. No converts, no confessions that Jesus is Lord; only increased animosity toward the followers of Jesus. But of course, this was far from the end of Stephen's influence and story, proven by this account being included in the Book of Acts. Someone witnessed Stephen's death and knew it mattered. Someone was impacted by what he said that day, by how he died that day with his faith firmly fixed on Christ. Likely, that someone was Paul, who partnered with Luke (the author of Acts) on many missionary ventures later in the book. It seems like Stephen's prayer for mercy for his persecutors found a most unlikely answer in the conversion of the ringleader of his execution.

Spirit-filled Christians find themselves doing many strange and wonderful things. Perhaps nothing is so strange and powerful as the fearlessness with which they can face suffering and death.

How have you experienced the Holy Spirit sustaining your faith in the midst of trials?

How have you seen faithful suffering encourage believers or open doors to sharing the gospel with unbelievers?

The Gospel Expands

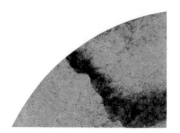

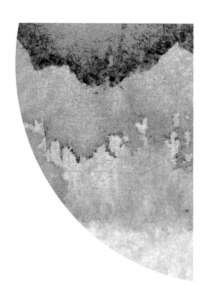

Introducing the Study

Jesus was clear in His command for the gospel to be shared in concentric circles, increasing in size. It would start in Jerusalem, then move to Judea, then Samaria, and finally to the ends of the earth. Despite the command, it took the death of Stephen, the first Christian martyr, for the church to move out from the confines of Jerusalem.

> How does Stephen's story motivate you, even if you are not being persecuted for your faith?

As a great wave of persecution crashed over the church in Jerusalem, the early Christians scattered, taking the gospel with them. Jesus had made it clear that the gospel was to be preached not only to the Jews in Judea but also to Gentiles across the world. As the Christians went out from Jerusalem, God was faithful to provide opportunities for them to speak the message of the gospel. And so, faith in Jesus began to transcend national and ethnic borders as God prepared the way.

 What are some ways God might prepare someone to hear the message of the gospel?

Setting the Context

The martyrdom of Stephen marked a significant escalation in the attacks against the early Christians and their gospel message. So severe was **the persecution** that all the Christians except the apostles scattered. Significantly, it's during this period of persecution that we are introduced to Saul, who approved of the killing of Stephen and emerged as the chief persecutor of the church.

Philip was one of the men appointed to take care of the needs of the church members. When the persecution began, Philip traveled to Samaria. The map on **"Expansion of the Early Church in Palestine"** (p. 35) traces the route Philip took after spreading out from the persecution in Jerusalem. Going to the Samaritans crossed a significant cultural line. Jews considered Samaritans as members of a lower class and as half-breeds because they descended from Jews who had intermarried with Gentiles

 What are some barriers in our own hearts that must come down so we can fulfill the Great Commission to make disciples of all nations?

Despite the cultural barriers, Philip proclaimed the gospel message to **the Samaritans**. God also used Philip to perform miracles in Samaria, which confirmed the truth of his message. Philip is the first missionary in the Book of Acts, but he would not be the last; he would be the first among many.

How does knowing that God might be at work preparing someone else to hear the gospel from you change your perspective of evangelism?

✝ CHRIST Connection

The Ethiopian eunuch was familiar with the Old Testament prophets but was unable to understand how their message was fulfilled in Jesus Christ. Philip was led by the Holy Spirit to help the eunuch understand how Jesus died on the cross for our sins and was raised from the dead, in accordance with the ancient prophecies.

Expansion of the
Early Church *in* Palestine

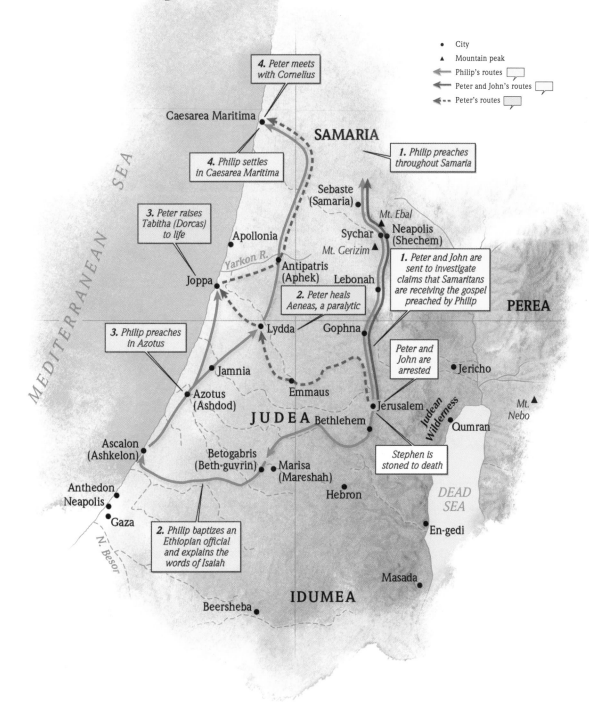

- • City
- ▲ Mountain peak
- ← Philip's routes
- ← Peter and John's routes
- ◄-- Peter's routes

4. Peter meets with Cornelius

Caesarea Maritima

SAMARIA

1. Philip preaches throughout Samaria

4. Philip settles in Caesarea Maritima

Sebaste (Samaria)

Mt. Ebal

3. Peter raises Tabitha (Dorcas) to life

Apollonia

Sychar

Neapolis (Shechem)

Mt. Gerizim

Yarkon R.

Antipatris (Aphek)

Lebonah

1. Peter and John are sent to investigate claims that Samaritans are receiving the gospel preached by Philip

PEREA

Joppa

2. Peter heals Aeneas, a paralytic

3. Philip preaches in Azotus

Lydda

Gophna

Peter and John are arrested

Jericho

Jamnia

Emmaus

Mt. Nebo

Azotus (Ashdod)

Jerusalem

Judean Wilderness

JUDEA Bethlehem

Qumran

Ascalon (Ashkelon)

Betogabris (Beth-guvrin)

Marisa (Mareshah)

Stephen is stoned to death

Anthedon Neapolis

Hebron

DEAD SEA

Gaza

2. Philip baptizes an Ethiopian official and explains the words of Isaiah

En-gedi

N. Besor

Masada

IDUMEA

Beersheba

MEDITERRANEAN SEA

Continuing the Discussion

 Watch this session's video, and then continue the group discussion using the following guide.

What does the story of Philip and the Ethiopian official show you about the character and purpose of God?

How, specifically, does this story encourage you in sharing your faith?

As a group, read Acts 8:26-29.

How would you describe Philip's response to the Spirit's instructions? What does this tell us about Philip?

How is Philip's situation similar to one you could experience?

Philip was living in a posture of obedient submission, so when the Spirit gave direction, he was ready to follow. Philip obeyed God's instruction and found a person in whom God had been at work. God has instructed us to share the gospel, and when we are obedient to this command, we too will find people in whom God has been preparing the way.

As a group, read Acts 8:30-35.

What might have happened had Philip been unprepared to talk about Scripture or been unfamiliar with Isaiah's prophecy?

What does this tell us about the connection between personal spiritual growth and spreading the good news of Jesus?

What can we learn from Philip's approach to sharing the gospel?

The Ethiopian was reading a prophecy from Isaiah concerning God's Suffering Servant, whom we know to be Jesus. When the man asked Philip to help him understand what he was reading, Philip was prepared and interpreted the passage, pointing the man to Jesus. In Philip's approach to sharing the gospel, we find a believer who was obedient to the leadership of the Holy Spirit, willing to approach people in real-life circumstances, and able to ask the right question and share the truth of the gospel.

As a group, read Acts 8:36-40.

 What did the man's question in verse 36 reveal?
How does this reflect a changed heart?

What does verse 40 teach us about Philip's continued faithfulness?

Philip's words were good news for the man because he believed the message of the gospel. His heart was changed, and Philip was obedient to Jesus' command to baptize those who come to faith. Then Philip was taken away miraculously—not taken by the Spirit *away from* ministry but *toward* new ministry. God had another appointment for Philip to share the gospel elsewhere.

✝ MISSIONAL Application

Record in this space at least one way you will apply the truth of Scripture as a recipient of God's grace communicated through His Word about Christ.

Personal Study 1

God's people are obedient to follow the Spirit's guidance.

Read Acts 8:26-29.

A thread runs throughout the Gospels and the Book of Acts that accentuates God's providence and planning. People find themselves prompted to hit the road, or they show up just in time to encounter Jesus or the apostles. This thread is at the core of Philip's story here in Acts 8. While Philip's encounter with the Ethiopian is rather brief, it is quite significant in the Book of Acts as it paints a picture of Spirit-prompted mission.

Consider this story's symbolic significance. Even though we don't think of Ethiopia as being far from Israel, in that day, the two regions were about as far apart as you could get from each other. To talk about Ethiopia would be like talking about the other side of the world. So in the minds of the original readers of Acts, the introduction of an Ethiopian to the story, especially one who had to come to Jerusalem in search of God, stood out. The Ethiopian reveals the global scope of the gospel message—it's a word for the nations, not just the Jews—and it shows us God's work to cultivate a hunger for Him in the hearts of all people.

The story of the Ethiopian reminds us that the Lord is working in the hearts of many to draw them to Himself, and they are responding. In this case, the Ethiopian knew enough to come to Jerusalem to look for Him, but in many cases, people will look wherever some semblance of hope and spirituality can be found.

If you look around, you can see this longing everywhere. It shows up in celebrity culture, where the promise of redemption and meaning gets packaged in the iconic pictures of models and stars. It shows up in politics, where people rally around leaders who promise hope, meaning, and a restoration of some lost glory. It shows up in all kinds of pseudo-religions, from fad diets to meditation practices, that promise youth, vitality, and inner peace. People rush to these transcendent promises because they're hungry.

Philip was sent by God for just such an encounter. Upon hearing the angel's command, Philip obeyed, dropped what he was doing and headed out on the road. There are many reasons for this encounter *not* to have happened. Philip had a good thing going in Samaria (8:4-8); he might have just stayed home and enjoyed the community he was already a part of. The Ethiopian might *not* have come to Jerusalem to worship God; there was surely no shortage of religious opportunity in Africa at the time.

Likewise, Philip might *not* have overcome the social anxiety that would likely have accompanied this encounter. Not only was the Ethiopian ethnically different from Philip, a hurdle significant enough at any point in history, but he was also of a higher social status than Philip. Luke tells us that he was a "high official of Candace, queen of the Ethiopians" (v. 27). Philip was an ordinary Jew living in Judea, a commoner; approaching someone of the Ethiopian's higher station wouldn't have been easy.

We could imagine a similar difficulty in approaching a celebrity or a high-level politician if we saw one in public. There's a certain resistance that's natural and a fear that accompanies it. We don't want to bother "important" people, and we don't want to offend them and invoke their ire either.

The Holy Spirit sent Philip despite all of these things, inviting him to overcome several layers of fear and resistance. His prompting ran against common-sense expectations, reminding us that the kingdom of God advances in surprising and counterintuitive ways.

What are some ways you've been surprised by how God has led you, your church, or your friends to be on mission?

How can we cultivate a heart willing to respond obediently to the Spirit's leading, no matter the risks?

Personal Study 2

God's people are faithful to show Jesus through the Scriptures.

Read Acts 8:30-35.

Philip approached the chariot and heard the Ethiopian reading the Scriptures, and found that God had already laid the groundwork for this encounter. The Ethiopian was immediately receptive to Philip, inviting him up onto the chariot to explain the Scriptures to him. Not only that, he *happened* to be reading a passage from the Book of Isaiah that overtly talks about the sacrificial death of Jesus. The whole conversation was teed up for Philip to point this man to Jesus.

Philip didn't have the credentials of a Bible scholar or a teacher of the law; again, he was an ordinary guy. But because he was filled with the Spirit and because of what he'd seen and experienced in his own life of faith, he responded with confidence and clarity.

The Bible can be an intimidating book for believers and unbelievers alike. For many readers, it's a dizzying collection of genres, languages, names, dates, and geographical locations. The connections between sections of the Bible—the Law, the Prophets, the Gospels, the Epistles—are often hard to draw out, and they often connect in ways that depend upon poetry, metaphor, and prophecy. For people lacking any background with the Bible, it can be overwhelming.

To make matters worse, there's no shortage of hucksters and swindlers who will use the Bible for their own selfish purposes. It's been used to justify the reign of despots, sustain the institution of slavery, and pad the pockets of innumerable criminals masquerading as pastors and evangelists. It's no wonder, then, that when Philip showed up at the side of the chariot, the Ethiopian lamented, "How can I [understand it] unless someone guides me?"

In the short passage that follows, we're given all we need to know about whether or not a Bible teacher is reliable. It's the simplest litmus test in the world, actually. They read a passage from Isaiah, and the Ethiopian invited Philip to explain it, asking whom the passage was about. And Philip "proceeded to tell him the good news about Jesus, beginning with that Scripture."

Bible teachers who are faithful to both their task and their text will always end up talking about Jesus. The whole story of the Bible, from one end to the other, points to Him. The story of Israel and the whole of the Old Testament are about anticipating Jesus. We see it in how they longed for a king, though all their kings fell short of the glory they aspired to. We see it in the high demands of the law, which no man can attain. We see it in the countless laments in the Psalms and Prophets, where the brokenness of the world is displayed and the people cry out, "How long, O Lord?"

Jesus manages to embody all that the Old Testament longs for and points to. Even the broader story of the Old Testament—exile from the garden of Eden, longing for the promised land, exile (again) at the hands of the Babylonians—points to Jesus as the conquering King who defeats Satan, sin, and death and brings us back home to God.

When we trust in Jesus, His Word and Spirit dwell in us, and we can see the ways that the Bible testifies to Him. Without that faith, we will struggle to make the connections. Philip's faith was his most important credential as a Bible teacher. His faith was what made him able and willing to follow the lead of the Spirit as he was sent here and there, and it was what made him able to hear God's Word and see Jesus in it.

Do you think it is possible to tell the good news about Jesus from anywhere in the Scriptures? Why or why not?

What are some reasons we might feel intimidated to explain the Scriptures to an unbeliever?

Personal Study 3

God's people are right to encourage faith in Christ.

Read Acts 8:36-40.

The Ethiopian official was moved by the story that Philip shared and was eager to respond. All of the elements of true conversion are on display here. The Ethiopian was eager to believe, not compelled, and certainly not pressured to convert. Philip had explained how the passage of Scripture he was reading pointed to Jesus, whose death and resurrection reconciles us to God. It seems he also explained enough so that the Ethiopian was eager to identify with Jesus through baptism.

"What would keep me from being baptized?" he asked. That question was crucial. Some might have offered a variety of reasons not to baptize him: he was an Ethiopian, not an ethnic Jew; he was a eunuch; he was a foreigner. He had just believed. But of course, Philip, filled with the Spirit, didn't put any stock in those hindrances. The Ethiopian believed what he had heard about Jesus—that He is the Lamb of God who takes away the sin of the world—and so, Philip baptized him without delay.

Evangelism and conversion really are that simple. We can share "just the facts," however, without asking people to make something of them. But the goal of evangelism isn't just to share what we know with people; it's to invite them to join us in following Jesus. The hope of an evangelist is to help someone see Jesus as Lord and that His life, death, and resurrection takes away the sins of the world and brings us home to God the Father. In Philip's short conversation with the Ethiopian, this miracle happened. He saw Jesus as Lord and was ready to follow Him into the waters of baptism.

As this story concludes, we see the two parted ways even more suddenly than they came together. What's implied here is that something more than meets the eye took Philip away. It's as if the Spirit carried him away and deposited him in Azotus. The Ethiopian, filled with the joy of being a new Christian and filled with the Holy Spirit, went on his own way back to his home, where one must imagine that the Spirit continued His work and the story of Jesus spread and grew roots in Africa.

The next leg in Philip's journey, though, continued his ministry of expanding the kingdom among the Gentiles. Azotus, where he suddenly appeared, was thirty miles away and wasn't a Jewish enclave. The kingdom's expansion to the non-Jewish world had officially begun.

It is always tempting to cling to spiritually rich, joy-filled moments. In Matthew 17, when Jesus allowed Peter, James, and John to witness His transfiguration and the appearance of Moses and Elijah, we see that temptation at work. Peter offered to build shelters for them, as if to say, "Let's just stay here and keep this thing going." Almost as soon as he said it, though, the moment ended—Jesus' physical appearance returned to normal and Moses and Elijah were gone.

This is a perfect metaphor for what we all experience in similar moments. There's a hunger to make the good times last, to stay put, to linger over what God has done. We feel it sometimes at the end of a retreat or in the midst of a rich worship experience, or we find ourselves looking back with a nostalgic fondness on moments like these in our past.

The Bible shows us that these moments, as rich as they are, are temporary. We are not meant to "stay put" in the past or even the present, but to keep moving forward. For Philip, ministry in Samaria was thriving, but the Lord called him away to meet the Ethiopian; he was then carried to Azotus and from there traveled on to Caesarea— but all the while, he was doing the work of an evangelist, calling people to believe in the good news of Jesus Christ.

How do the details of this story fulfill Jesus' Great Commission to His disciples (Matt. 28:18-20)?

Why is calling for a response vital when sharing the gospel of Jesus Christ with others?

Saul Is Saved

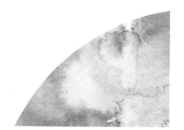

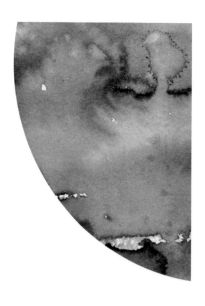
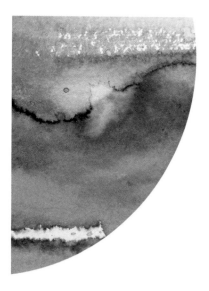

Introducing the Study

As He did with Joseph being sold into slavery in Egypt, God took the death of Stephen, what others intended for evil, and used it for good. Though the Jewish officials put Stephen to death to strike fear into the fledgling Christian movement and stamp it out, their violence scattered the church, pushing the Christian message out of Jerusalem into other areas. They unknowingly contributed to God's redemptive plan of blessing every nation with the gospel.

 **How might our perspective of suffering change when we consider God's broader plan of redemption?**

The gospel was on the move, yet persecution continued. One of the main perpetrators of that persecution was a young Pharisee named Saul. Bent on destroying what he saw as blasphemy to the religion he loved, Saul was tireless in his efforts to seek out and imprison Christians. But here again we see God's unexpected work and unmerited grace take hold. Saul had a great role to play in God's ongoing story of redemption.

Who are some people or groups of people we might consider beyond the reach of God's saving grace?

Setting the Context

The Bible first introduces us to **Saul at the stoning of Stephen**. Saul was at least a cheering bystander, if not an active participant, during the first Christian martyrdom. Saul was a Roman citizen, born in Tarsus of Cilicia. But according to his own testimony, he was brought up in an idealistically Jewish fashion. His parents were Pharisees, strict adherents to the law. Being brought up in this environment, Saul was staunchly religious, holding himself and others to the highest legal standard. As **a strict Jew**, Saul refused to associate with anything unclean, especially Gentiles.

 How would Saul's refusal to associate with Gentiles correspond to God's law? To God's heart?

As a young man, Saul lived in Jerusalem and learned from an esteemed rabbi named Gamaliel. Saul's education would have included years of studying Jewish history, the Psalms, and the writings of the prophets.

As a Pharisee, Saul saw Christianity as blasphemy. The idea that God could become a man was, in his mind, an affront to the holiness of Yahweh. So severe was this offense that Saul believed it should be punishable by death, as it was with Stephen, so he made it his life's mission to root out other Christians. But God had a different future in mind for Saul, which would involve him going by his Greek name. **"Paul's Life"** (p. 47) provides an overview of that future.

What do stories of salvation—all of which are miraculous—teach us about the heart of God and the power of the gospel?

✝ CHRIST Connection

The conversion and calling of Saul is a demonstration of God's power to save. Through an encounter with the crucified and risen Jesus, this once-hardened persecutor of God's people began his journey to becoming the greatest missionary the world has ever known. Only the gospel can transform a public opponent of Christ into a fervent witness to His salvation.

Paul's *Life*

THE PHARISEE

- A Jew born in Tarsus but trained in Jerusalem by Gamaliel; zealous for God (Acts 22:3)
- Agreed with the stoning of Stephen and persecuted the church; traveled to Damascus to arrest believers and bring them back to Jerusalem (7:58; 8:1,3; 9:1-2; 22:4-5)

THE CHRISTIAN

- Met Jesus on the way to Damascus and was blinded; three days later, he was healed by Ananias so he could see, filled with the Holy Spirit, and baptized (9:3-18)
- Proclaimed Jesus in the synagogues in Damascus, and later in Jerusalem (9:20-30)
- Found by Barnabas in Tarsus; taken to Antioch to help teach the disciples (11:25-26)

THE MISSIONARY

- Saul and Barnabas set apart by the Spirit for missionary calling (13:1-3)
- FIRST MISSIONARY JOURNEY (13:4–14:28)
- Saul sent with Barnabas to the Jerusalem Council, which discussed and affirmed salvation by faith for Gentiles (15:1-35)
- SECOND MISSIONARY JOURNEY (15:36–18:22)
- THIRD MISSIONARY JOURNEY (18:23–21:19)
- Arrested in Jerusalem; defended his faith before kings and rulers; appealed to Caesar and sent to Rome, where he proclaimed Jesus while under house arrest (21:26–28:31)
- According to tradition, released from house arrest but then arrested a second time and imprisoned in Rome, and later beheaded

Continuing the Discussion

▶ Watch this session's video, and then continue the group discussion using the following guide.

What is your biggest takeaway when you think about the conversion of Saul?

In what ways should Saul's encounter with Jesus encourage us in sharing our own faith?

As a group, read Acts 9:3-9.

✻ What might Jesus have wanted to teach Saul through his blindness?

Given his background, what might Saul have been thinking about during those three days of blindness and fasting?

Jesus didn't ask Saul why he was persecuting the church but Him personally. This is not because He does not care for the church; instead, Christ so identifies with His followers that to attack them is to attack Him. Jesus revealed Himself to Saul and gave him instructions, which Saul followed immediately. Saul's fasting and blindness were not punishment but an appropriate response to the intensity of his encounter with Jesus. Just as he was blind spiritually, he was struck blind physically. But God would lift both forms of blindness.

As a group, read Acts 9:10-16.

How do you think Ananias felt when the Lord instructed him to take care of Saul?

✻ What does God's plan for Saul reveal about His power and purposes?

Ananias's response of "Here I am, Lord" revealed a heart that was eager to please the Lord and obey Him. Where most Christians would have looked at Saul with warranted fear and trepidation, God wanted Ananias to see a "chosen instrument" He would use to carry the gospel to the known world. We must not write off anyone, even those who are hostile to the faith, because God's power in the gospel can melt even the hardest heart.

As a group, read Acts 9:17-20.

 What is significant about the way Ananias addressed Saul?

What does Ananias's response to God's direction reveal about his faith?

What stands out to you about what Saul did shortly after being baptized?

God could have healed Saul without the personal interaction with another believer, but God has never intended anyone to live for Him apart from the fellowship of the church. When Ananias addressed Saul as brother, he was affirming Saul's new relationship with the church. He was no longer a persecutor of the faith; he was now part of the family of faith. After Saul was baptized, he began proclaiming the One he had scorned. Though Saul might not have known everything about following Christ, he knew enough to begin sharing the gospel with those around him.

✟ MISSIONAL Application

Record in this space at least one way you will apply the truth of Scripture as one whose hardened heart has been changed by Jesus.

Personal Study 1

Saul is confronted by the Savior.

Read Acts 9:3-9.

Saul was deeply disturbed. A start-up band of blasphemous followers of a rebellious Rabbi named Jesus was claiming He had been resurrected from the dead. It was ludicrous, and yet the movement was growing. This talk of Jesus being the resurrected Son of God needed to be stopped. So Saul set out with his colleagues on a hunt to find, persecute, and eradicate all who were allegiant to Jesus of Nazareth.

Stephen's death had driven those who loved Christ into deep mourning and also scattered them throughout the region (Acts 8:1-2). For those fleeing Jerusalem, Damascus would have been one of the closest major towns just a few days travel away. When Jesus' disciples scattered, Saul eyed the nearby city as a likely destination for many of them. Seeing the opportunity to continue his campaign to eradicate the church, Saul's fury turned from Jerusalem toward Damascus.

As Saul approached Damascus, he was most likely considering how he would capture and eliminate those who followed Christ in the city. But he would not do the capturing that day; instead he would be the one captured. His capture began in the form of a bright light and a question.

"Saul, Saul, why are you persecuting me?" The question confounded Saul. He did not recognize the voice as coming from Jesus because he did not know Jesus. But Saul knew it was a divine messenger whom he needed to heed with reverence. But why would an angelic messenger from the one true God confront him about his righteous effort to get rid of those blaspheming God? Saul wasn't persecuting God; he was trying to serve Him! The Pharisee couldn't answer the divine messenger's perplexing question, so he responded with a question of his own: "Who are you, Lord?"

Jesus identified Himself as the One being persecuted because Saul was persecuting His followers. What Saul was doing to the disciples he was actually doing to Christ Himself. At this moment, humiliation and humility began to set in. The world as Paul knew it was about to change, and the world as we now know it was about to begin its formation. Saul's marching orders from the high priest were about to be usurped by orders from the Great High Priest—"go into the city, and you will be told what you must do." Sounds simple enough, but it was easier said than done.

Luke, described Saul this way: "though his eyes were open, he could see nothing," a clear reference back to the teachings of Jesus when He had called the Jewish religious leaders "blind guides" in Matthew 23.

If you have been "churched" your whole life, beware. It is easy to become convinced your religious ways are the same as Christ's ways when instead they are actually opposed to His righteous purposes. Jesus doesn't confront us to produce superficial, religious obedience. That was what Saul excelled at before his confrontation. Instead, Jesus confronts us to show who He is and to transform our hearts, leading to loving, genuine obedience. Jesus' encounter with Saul shows that He can soften even the hardest hearts of people full of themselves.

God used a pretty unique confrontation with Saul to get his attention. In what ways do you see Jesus confronting people today?

What are some ways we can be blind and confuse religious obedience with what truly pleases God?

Personal Study 2

Saul is called for a mission.

Read Acts 9:10-16.

God making surprising choices is a consistent theme throughout Scripture. When God chose someone to make into a great nation, he chose Abraham, a man with a wife who could not have children. Then when God continued His covenant through the descendants of Abraham, He chose to do so through the younger brother, Jacob, rather than the older one, Esau. Later, when God chose a new king for the nation of Israel, He chose David, who didn't look like a king or have the right pedigree. And when God chose to send His Son to be born as a baby, He chose for that birth to happen in a stable and for common shepherds to be the first witnesses to the Rescuer's arrival. God works in surprising ways through surprising people.

So perhaps we should not be surprised when God once again made a surprising choice for whom He would send to take the gospel to the Gentiles. He chose Saul, the last person anyone would have expected. No one could have predicted that Saul, the ardent persecutor of the church, would become one of her greatest champions and heralds. That included a man named Ananias.

Put yourself in Ananias' position for a moment. Surely he was excited to hear the voice of the Lord and he was eager to obey. Notice the difference in how Saul and Ananias responded to the Lord. Saul wanted to know who He was; Ananias wanted to know how he could serve Him. "Here I am, Lord," Ananias declared, unaware of the great risk God was about to call on him to take. The instructions were straightforward, though. Ananias was to go to Straight Street to the house of Judas to give marching orders from Jesus to Saul.

Saul—the persecutor, imprisoner, and murderer of people like Ananias. Jesus said Saul would be expecting him. Ananias began processing this baffling instruction from God. His fellow Christ-followers and he had heard of Saul and no one was planning on having breakfast with him any time soon.

Ananias' reply was basically, "Maybe you have the wrong guy and wrong address, Lord." But Ananias was not trying to question the authority of Jesus; he wanted to understand why Jesus would call on him to run straight toward danger. It was difficult to understand. But Jesus was adamant: "Go." Ananias was to step out in faith and serve the man who had come to his city to kill him.

But God's instructions were not without explanation. God assured Ananias that Saul had a pivotal role to play in God's story of redemption. This man—the one responsible for the reign of terror that had fallen on the church—would experience such a radical transformation that he would be an instrument of the gospel. Before he had spread fear; now he would proclaim forgiveness. He had been a champion of the law; now he would preach grace. He had believed Gentiles to be unclean; now he would welcome them into the kingdom. And he had inflicted suffering because of Christ; now he would suffer for Christ. Saul was to be sent out on mission, and it was a mission he never expected.

So Ananias obeyed and his heart was opened to a man who should have been his enemy but who was now his brother. And at the same time, Saul's eyes were opened to the gospel of Jesus, he was filled with the Holy Spirit, and he was baptized as the sign of being a true disciple of Jesus. The Christ-persecutor was now a Christ-follower. Saul, like Ananias, was now called on to step out in faith to share the gospel, even when things would come full circle and he would be persecuted for his faith (Acts 9:16). We should all be grateful for the obedience of Ananias, the Damascus resident whom God used to encourage the man who would become perhaps the greatest missionary and theologian of the church.

We normally think of God sending us to share the gospel with unbelievers. How does God send us to other believers too?

How have other believers come alongside you like Ananias did for Saul?

Personal Study 3

Saul is united with other believers.

Read Acts 9:17-20.

There is one word that must have made all the difference for Saul. There he was, blinded physically, and coming to understand the extent of his spiritual blindness. Then there was a knock on the door of the little room where he had sat for the past three days without eating or drinking. And that's when he heard the word: "brother."

How sweet that word must have been to the ears of the blind man. How he must have perked up when he heard it. This word was followed by an explanation that the person behind the voice he heard had come on behalf of Jesus, the One who had appeared to Saul on the road, so that his sight might be regained and that he would be filled with the Holy Spirit. There was not an "I-told-you-so" tone of arrogance accompanying what he heard. What he heard was not a word of judgment. Instead, it was a word of grace. Jesus had sent someone to speak truth into the confusion that had become Saul's life.

This interaction was the launching pad Saul needed. Something like scales fell from his eyes and he could physically see again, but more importantly, he was also beginning to see spiritually with vivid clarity. After, Saul went where he had originally planned to go—the synagogues—but with a much different message: "He is the Son of God." Imagine the surprise of those who knew of Saul, the zealous persecutor of the church, when they heard him proclaim the very thing that had been grounds to execute Stephen.

Furthermore, imagine the surprise of the Jews who were beginning to believe Jesus was the Messiah because of the message from this fledgling preacher whom Jesus had just confronted. Saul preaching Jesus confounded the Jews (Acts 9:22), meaning, Saul was so convincing and clear that his listeners were at a loss as to how to refute him.

If we keep on reading in Acts, we see that Saul eventually made his way to Jerusalem. When he got there, he was met with suspicion. After all, this was the same man who had been breathing down the neck of the fledgling church. But here again we find another Christian willing to stand up and vouch for the new convert. This time it was Barnabas, whose name means "son of encouragement." Barnabas endorsed Saul, which served to encourage him in his mission.

In both of these cases, God used the fellowship of Christians to solidify and perpetuate Saul's calling. The same thing happens today. It is often through the church that we discover how God has uniquely gifted us to proclaim and demonstrate the gospel, and it's through the church that we find the necessary encouragement to persevere in that calling.

While not all of us are called to be Paul, we are all called to be Ananias. We are all, as part of God's fellowship of believers, meant to be the ones who offer support and encourage others. We are meant to be looking—and looking with expectation— for where the sovereign hand of God has positioned us. We might not ever gain the notoriety of Paul, but we must move toward the spirit of Ananias. In doing so, we must approach every single interaction, no matter how common and ordinary it might seem, with the same words that characterized this great supporting character in the biopic of the apostle: "Here I am, Lord."

Who has served in the role of Ananias or Barnabas for you?

What are some of the obstacles you encounter in serving others as Ananias or Barnabas did?

The Mission Is Embraced

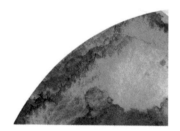
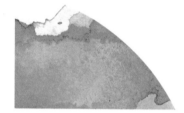

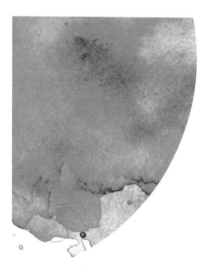

Introducing the Study

There is no such thing as a lost cause to God. For a time, Saul was Christianity's greatest opponent, but after an encounter with the crucified and risen Jesus, he became its greatest apologist and defender. He once sought to imprison Christians, but later he would end up in prison for preaching Christ himself. This could only happen because of the power of the gospel, which can transform even the hardest heart.

 Why is it important for us as Christians to recognize that the gospel can transform the hardest of hearts?

Jesus told His disciples that they were to be His witnesses first in Jerusalem and then into Judea, Samaria, and all of the world. This expansion began with disciples like Philip and continued through the conversion of Saul. But they were just the beginning. The New Testament church would soon embrace her role as both witness and sending agent to complete the mission God had given her through Jesus.

What are some ways Christians participate in the global mission of the church?

Setting the Context

God was clear that the gospel was not a message for the Jews alone. It was to start with the Jews but not end with them—it was to go to the very ends of the earth. Later, God told Ananias that **Saul, also known as Paul**, would be His chosen instrument to deliver the message of the gospel not only to the Jews but also to the Gentiles. Jesus provided salvation for the entire world; thus, the gospel is a message of hope that crosses all national, political, ethnic, and cultural boundaries.

> **How have we already seen God's work, salvation, and glory reach out to the nations in the pages of Scripture?**

As the Book of Acts continues, the church grows in her understanding of this key truth. **Peter**, for example, was given a vision from God that was followed by a divine appointment with a Gentile named Cornelius. Peter came to understand that he should proclaim the good news of the gospel to anyone who would hear.

Meanwhile, the gospel was spread by those who had been scattered after Stephen's martyrdom. **The church in Antioch** became the first multiethnic congregation and would soon give birth to the first great missionary-sending movement of the church, represented by **"The First Missionary Journey of Paul"** (p. 59).

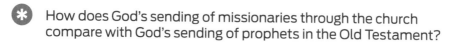 **How does God's sending of missionaries through the church compare with God's sending of prophets in the Old Testament?**

✝ CHRIST Connection

Jesus told His disciples that the gates of hell would not prevail against His church, reminding us that God's people are "on offense," continuing the mission Jesus began. God's plan is for Christians to take the powerful and good news of Jesus to places of deep spiritual darkness with full confidence that Jesus will build His church.

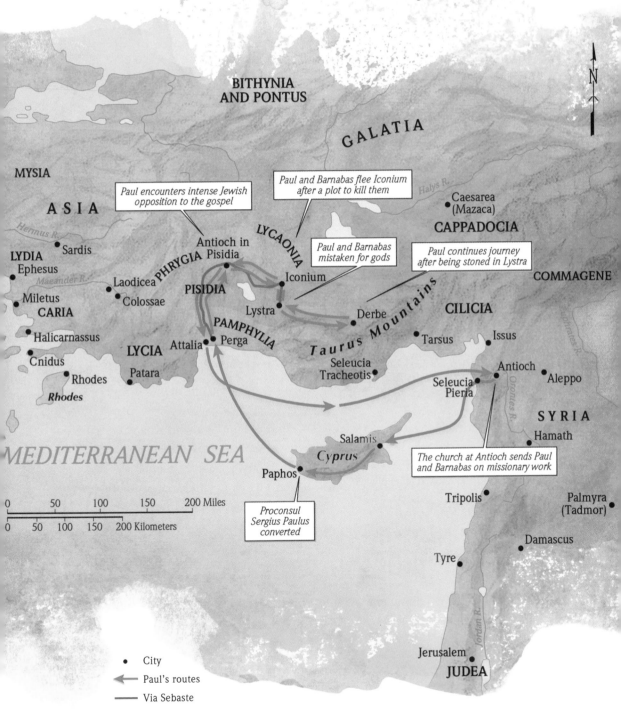

The First
Missionary Journey *of* Paul

N

BITHYNIA
AND PONTUS

GALATIA

MYSIA

ASIA

Hermus R.

LYDIA

Sardis

Ephesus

Maeander R.

Laodicea

Colossae

PHRYGIA

Miletus

CARIA

Halicarnassus

Cnidus

Rhodes

Rhodes

LYCIA

Attalia

Patara

PAMPHYLIA

Perga

Antioch in
Pisidia

PISIDIA

Lystra

Paul encounters intense Jewish
opposition to the gospel

LYCAONIA

Iconium

Paul and Barnabas flee Iconium
after a plot to kill them

Paul and Barnabas
mistaken for gods

Derbe

Taurus Mountains

Seleucia
Tracheotis

Halys R.

Caesarea
(Mazaca)

CAPPADOCIA

Paul continues journey
after being stoned in Lystra

COMMAGENE

CILICIA

Tarsus

Issus

Antioch

Aleppo

Seleucia
Pieria

Orontes R.

SYRIA

Hamath

MEDITERRANEAN SEA

Salamis

Cyprus

Paphos

The church at Antioch sends Paul
and Barnabas on missionary work

Proconsul
Sergius Paulus
converted

Tripolis

Palmyra
(Tadmor)

Damascus

Tyre

Jordan R.

0   50   100   150   200 Miles

0   50   100   150   200 Kilometers

•   City

⟵   Paul's routes

———   Via Sebaste

Jerusalem

JUDEA

Continuing the Discussion

▶ Watch this session's video, and then continue the group discussion using the following guide.

What is the role of the Holy Spirit in the church and in missionaries?

Why might some Jewish believers have been reluctant to share the gospel with Gentiles and to embrace Gentile believers?

As a group, read Acts 13:1-3.

✳ How would you describe the priorities of the church at Antioch based on these verses?

What were some of the reasons the church could have given for not sending out Saul and Barnabas?

Why do you think it was important for the missionaries to have a church as a sending base?

The church at Antioch heard from the Lord—He called out Saul and Barnabas for His special work. Though they might have hesitated sending two of their key leaders, the church was determined to live out God's mission and trusted Him in faith. The church at Antioch played an important role in commissioning and supporting these two missionaries whom the Lord had called, which would launch a great expansion of the church.

As a group, read Acts 13:4-8.

✳ How would you describe the missionaries' ministry philosophy based on these verses?

Is it right to expect opposition when we proclaim the gospel? Why or why not?

Establishing their method of evangelism, Saul and Barnabas went to the synagogue to proclaim the gospel, but they didn't stop there. They were willing to share with anyone who was willing to hear. But not all were willing. The gospel was met with some opposition. Likewise, we should be prepared for opposition because of the exclusive nature of the gospel message we proclaim.

As a group, read Acts 13:9-12.

 What purpose did the miracle of judgment serve in this passage?

How is this consistent with the purpose of miracles in the ministry of Jesus?

These missionaries had the same priorities as their Lord. Their greatest aim was for the gospel to be preached and believed. As was the case with Jesus, the miraculous signs served to validate the truth of the message of the gospel. People would see the power of the gospel, giving credibility to the gospel they heard.

✝ MISSIONAL Application

Record in this space at least one way you will apply the truth of Scripture as one who has benefited from the missionary efforts of Jesus' disciples.

Personal Study 1

God raises missionaries from within the church.

Read Acts 13:1-3.

After Saul's conversion recorded in Acts 9, he is not mentioned for a few chapters and Peter takes center stage in the book once again. Then, Saul re-emerges at the end of Acts 12 when he returns to Jerusalem along with Barnabas and Mark. The men had been on a relief mission because of the famine that had spread across the empire (Acts 11:27-30).

Somehow Saul (later Paul) and Barnabas end up in close fellowship with the church at Antioch. There God called these two men and set them apart for His righteous purposes—the first recorded missionary journey in Scripture. This missionary journey would span eight cities in several regions of the eastern portion of the Roman Empire, laying the foundation for two other missionary journeys to follow and eventually Paul delivering the gospel to Rome.

The church at Antioch was wonderfully diverse as several different ethnic groups were represented among its leaders. Following the stoning of Stephen, the early church had taken the gospel of Jesus from Jerusalem to Judea into Samaria and was now beginning to go to the ends of the earth (Acts 1:8). The results were already noticeable, but the work was just beginning.

As the leaders were worshiping and fasting, they heard from the Holy Spirit. It might be easy to read past this important connection between practicing these spiritual disciplines and being tuned in to the Holy Spirit, but it deserves our attention. These leaders and the church with them were in the right posture to hear from God and then respond accordingly when the time came.

The Holy Spirit instructed the church to set apart Barnabas and Saul for the work to which God had called them. God was separating these two men from the normal rhythms of being part of the church at Antioch for something else. Barnabas and Saul would leave their church, and their lives as they knew them, to advance the gospel to unreached regions as missionaries.

After the leaders fasted, prayed, and laid hands on the pair in recognition and affirmation of God's calling, they sent them off. The word used here is a word that carries the idea of far more than a casual goodbye. This sending was a stronger separation. The word can also be translated "divorce." It was a tearing apart of a Christ-formed family, but in the context of the mission of God, it was a Christ-approved severing.

This division certainly hurt. Sending is never easy. That was true for the church in Antioch then, and it is true of our churches today. When churches send, they lose vital people and resources for the work where they are. Sending is hard, painful, and risky.

Being sent isn't any easier. Going with God into a new, often unknown land as a missionary is hard, especially because of the family we leave behind, both biological and spiritual.

So why go if the pain is so great? It's because the good news of the gospel that we believe is greater. The gospel compels us to go and help others believe it too. It calls us to give drink for the thirsty, nourishment for the hungry, medicine for the sick, friendship for the imprisoned, clothes for the cold, security for the orphan, help for the widow, and hope for all through the message of the gospel. We ought to do these things out of human decency, but deeper than that, for the Christian, we are compelled to act in these ways because of what Jesus has done for us.

How do you support missionaries sent by your local church?

What are some common reasons people might offer as their justification for not going as missionaries themselves?

Personal Study 2

God guides missionaries to proclaim the gospel.

Read Acts 13:4-8.

The missionaries were off, bolstered by a church that no doubt continued to pray for them and their mission. Saul and Barnabas made the sixteen-mile journey to Seleucia and then boarded a boat to sail to Cyprus. When they landed, they followed what had become their typical method of evangelism: go to a city, start in the synagogue, and then move out from there.

It was a simple plan. But the reason a plan like this could be so simple, and yet so effective, is because it was predicated on faith. So what did Saul and Barnabas believe to take this pathway of ministry? First, they believed the gospel was for all people. Having come from Antioch, they had seen the gospel's power to break down walls typical in society. Jews and Gentiles did not speak to each other, much less fellowship together, but they had seen a congregation united by the blood of Jesus.

They also believed that the Holy Spirit would pave the way for the gospel message they would proclaim. Saul and Barnabas were not about to preach their opinions or philosophies; they were about to preach the message of the gospel. They were witnesses to the death and resurrection of Jesus, and because this was their message, they could be confident what they shared was in the center of God's will.

Finally they believed in the power of the gospel. Saul was a walking testimony to this power. It had not been that long since Saul had been on the other side of the faith, making it his life's mission to root out and destroy Christianity. And yet here he was in Cyprus of all places, a former Pharisee of Pharisees now proclaiming that Jesus Christ is Lord. The gospel has power to transform the hardest of hearts, and so they could proclaim this message with great confidence. And that is exactly what they did.

So Saul and Barnabas headed across the island declaring the message to any who would listen, until they ran across a false prophet. This man served as an attendant of the Roman proconsul who wanted to hear the word of God. But Elymas the sorcerer did not want that to happen; he wanted to turn the proconsul away from the gospel message. We should not be surprised.

Just because God guides us to share the gospel, we should not expect the road in doing so to be without opposition. That's because the gospel, by its very nature, is divisive. Think for a moment about what people must accept when they hear the message of Jesus.

They must accept the news about themselves that they are sinners, dead in their own sin. They must accept that they cannot do anything to change this condition and instead are at the mercy of God. Then they must accept that Jesus loves them enough to die in their place, though they do not deserve it. And they must accept that Jesus rose from the dead, nonsense to the world. These are difficult truths, but they are an all-or-nothing proposition.

This brings us back to the core of what we believe. Perhaps our failure to share the gospel is, many times, less about our preparation, and more an indictment on our own confidence in the power of the message we are to proclaim. Do we really believe the truth of the gospel? If we do, then we will be witnesses to the power of God through that message.

When have you seen the power of God through the gospel change someone's heart?

In what sense does your willingness to share the gospel validate your own belief in the gospel?

Personal Study 3

God gives missionaries power to validate the gospel.

Read Acts 13:9-12.

The missionaries experienced mixed results in their first stop in Cyprus. On the one hand, they encountered an important Roman official eager to hear the Word of God. On the other hand they also encountered a false prophet who felt threatened by the gospel and was determined to put a stop to it.

But Saul—also called Paul—would not be intimidated. And why should he be? Here was a man who was spiritually blind to the truth of God, just as Paul was. And Paul knew how that ended up. So Paul, empowered by the Holy Spirit, confronted the man. The false prophet was called "Bar-Jesus", which means "son of the Savior." Paul seized on the name and told the truth. This man was no son of the Savior—he was a son of the devil. As such, he was standing against the power and will of God. But he was about to experience just how powerful the one true God is.

Perhaps Paul remembered his own experience as he pronounced the Lord's judgment on the false prophet, and the man was struck blind. The Roman proconsul, meanwhile, heard the teaching, saw the sign, and believed.

It's important for us to see how these things worked together because even today there are those who tread on the name of Jesus for the supposed benefits He can provide. There are those who promise miraculous healings, financial prosperity, and a secure physical wellness in the name of Jesus. And yet that's not how we see the preaching and the miraculous sign working in this passage.

Paul and Barnabas understood that their primary mission was centered on the gospel message. They were, first and foremost, to be witnesses to the life, death, and resurrection of Christ. If that was their goal, then everything else must contribute to that goal. In other words, there were no isolated miracles, no random signs. Rather, the miraculous good that happened through these missionaries served the greater purpose of validating the message.

The same thing was true in the ministry of Jesus. Jesus healed many who were in need that came to Him. Yes, He cared for these people. He had compassion for them. But He healed them for another reason—as a means to the greater end of faith in His identity and message.

What we find here, then, is a paradigm for how the message of the gospel and gospel-compelled actions work together. It is good and right for us to pursue the common good of mankind. We should by all means give our resources and our lives for the purpose of meeting the needs of the world around us. Christians ought to lead the way in issues of social justice and the common good. But doing these things serves the greater purpose of spreading the gospel. This is our mission; this is our end.

We serve those in need, care for those who hurt, and provide for those who lack so they might come to know and understand the gospel. This is what compels us forward. And these acts are often what validates the message that accompanies them.

Why is it essential for us to understand the primary task of speaking the message of the gospel?

What happens to our witness if we fail to keep the proclamation of the gospel central to our mission?

The Gospel Is Clarified

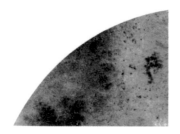
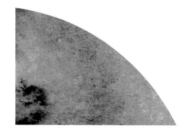
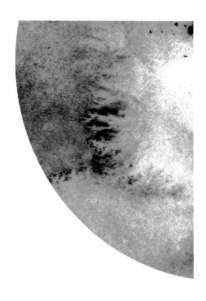
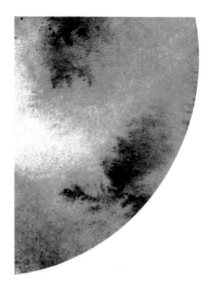

Introducing the Study

The church was young, but it was already changing. What began as a primarily Jewish congregation in Jerusalem was morphing into a multiethnic, multinational people. Furthermore, the church was embracing her mission not only to gather but also to scatter. Individual churches, like Antioch, became sending points for missionaries to carry the gospel message to the ends of the earth.

 How should we pray for the church in light of what we have seen from the church at Antioch?

Missionaries like Barnabas and Paul, along with many others, were spreading throughout the world and taking the message of the gospel with them. With more and more people from different and diverse backgrounds embracing the gospel, the church was at a critical point. The young church was growing and flourishing, but that same growth could threaten the church's foundation—the gospel of Jesus. The leaders of the church had to define the core aspects of the gospel message to protect it for all time.

Why might rapid expansion have caused the need for the church leaders to clarify the nature of the gospel?

Setting the Context

Paul and Barnabas had been sent by the church at Antioch on their **first missionary journey**. As they traveled, they shared the gospel, planted churches, appointed leaders, and entrusted the care of these new congregations to them. All in all, it was an enormously successful trip. The gospel was flourishing among the Gentiles. Churches had been started. The kingdom was expanding to include people of every tribe, language, and nation.

> How would the churches Paul and Barnabas planted serve as outposts or embassies of God's kingdom in foreign lands?

After they returned to their home base of Antioch, they celebrated with the church all that God was doing among the Gentiles. But soon they were dragged into a dispute that centered on the Jewish rite of **circumcision**. For centuries, circumcision was the mark that identified the people of God from the rest of the nations. Many circumcised Jews had become Christians, and some of these men came to Antioch to teach that Gentiles coming to faith in Christ must be circumcised to be saved.

A serious argument broke out regarding the nature of the gospel. Looking at **"The Big Picture"** (p. 71), the debate was over the requirements for redemption in Christ. The church had come to a pivotal moment, one that would not only clarify the gospel but also set the course for the expansion of the Christian witness in the future.

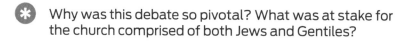 Why was this debate so pivotal? What was at stake for the church comprised of both Jews and Gentiles?

✝ CHRIST Connection

The Jerusalem Council met to resolve a dispute in the early church: Was faith in Christ sufficient for salvation and inclusion into God's family or was something else needed? The early church's response affirmed the sufficiency of faith in Jesus for salvation. Because of His finished work on the cross, Jesus alone is all we need to be saved.

The **Big Picture**

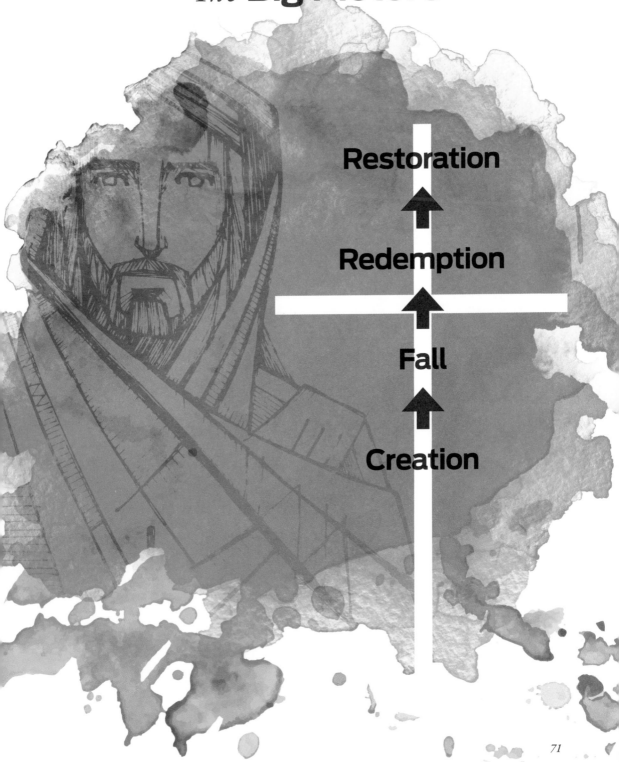

Restoration

Redemption

Fall

Creation

Continuing the Discussion

▶ Watch this session's video, and then continue the group discussion using the following guide.

Why is it so dangerous to add anything to the message of the gospel, as these Jewish teachers were trying to do at Antioch?

What are some ways we can make sure the gospel we share remains pure?

As a group, read Acts 15:1-5.

How might people in the church today impose further regulation on the message of the gospel?

Why do you think Paul disagreed so sharply with these teachers?

✱ What was the core of the issue, if not the specific act of circumcision?

The first-century church was a melting pot of converts. Both Jews and Gentiles were becoming followers of Jesus. While the Gentiles shared no cultural history with the Jews and didn't know their spiritual history as a nation, the Jews wanted the new Gentile converts to follow many of the Old Testament laws that had been in place for centuries in order to find acceptance with God. Yet they'd already found acceptance in Christ—there was nothing left to do.

As a group, read Acts 15:6-18.

How would you explain Peter's argument?

✱ Why was the Holy Spirit a critical part of this discussion?

The apostle Peter turned the conversation to the main point: Salvation is all about God's grace to the sinner. No one is saved by good works. Peter reminded his audience that the weight of evidence was against justification coming through works—his own people had tried to live up to the law for centuries but failed. Further, God had given the Gentiles the gift of the Spirit, which validated their salvation by faith alone.

As a group, read Acts 15:19-21.

 What is the significance of the council's decision in light of Acts 1:8?

How did this decision pave the way for the future of Christian expansion?

James, the leader of the Jerusalem church, spoke up at the meeting of the Jerusalem Council. He believed that adding the requirements of the Mosaic law would hinder the new Gentile believers. The evidence was incontrovertible: God had turned His attention and grace to the Gentiles by faith, just as He had the Jews. The decision not only clarified the gospel, it also fell squarely in line with Jesus' instructions to the church.

✝ MISSIONAL Application

Record in this space at least one way you will apply the truth of Scripture as a sinner saved by grace alone through faith alone in Christ alone.

Personal Study 1

The Dispute: "Jesus Alone" vs. "Jesus Plus"

Read Acts 15:1-5.

Just before this in Acts 13–14, we see how the early church had sent the missionaries Paul and Barnabas to push the gospel farther out from Jerusalem as Jesus had instructed (Acts 1:8). The trip had been difficult for the two missionaries, but many had come to faith in Christ, including a number of Gentiles. News spread of what God had done, but not everyone in the church who heard it was pleased. As Paul and Barnabas made their way back to Antioch, trouble was brewing.

The dispute began when some men who evidently had heard the reports of Gentiles coming to faith in Christ came from Judea to Antioch. The men did not deny the possibility of Gentiles being saved; they denied the possibility of anyone being saved apart from obedience to the law. Notice that when the men arrived, they began to teach that circumcision was necessary for salvation.

We are not told that these men from Judea investigated the reports of Gentiles coming to faith to see if they were true; it seems they assumed that the reports could not have been true because of their unwavering allegiance to their cultural customs and religious traditions. A significant part of the identity of these men had been based on their allegiance to the Law of Moses—the way they were set apart as God's people from the nations around them—and this was difficult for them to give up: *if circumcision had been a critical aspect of the identity of God's people before Christ, why would it not be now?*

When Paul and Barnabas heard what the men were teaching, they confronted them and engaged them in serious argument and debate. The crux of the debate can be boiled down to the question of whether Jesus alone is sufficient for salvation or if something else—anything else, such as circumcision in this case—was needed in addition. Paul and Barnabas objected to the teachings of these men for two probable reasons.

The primary reason centered on the core of the gospel—salvation by grace alone through faith alone (Eph. 2:8-9). The men from Judea were teaching that faith alone was not sufficient for salvation; instead, a person first had to belong to God's covenant community, the people of Israel, and becoming part of that community required the mark of circumcision. Paul and Barnabas understood that you did not have to be part of the right people before you could be saved but that anyone anywhere can be saved in the moment they trust in Jesus Christ.

Requiring a Gentile to be circumcised first would mean that they had to do something first to earn the right to be saved, but no one is worthy to be saved. No one deserves an invitation into a relationship with the living God. Salvation is by grace. Grace initiated it. Grace sustains it. Grace fulfills it. Gentiles should not have to do something to earn salvation when no one else had done anything to merit it.

A second related reason Paul and Barnabas confronted the men from Judea might have been linked to their missionary hearts. Most missionaries look to engage people right where they are as they encourage them to consider the gospel. Requiring circumcision of the Gentiles would be an added burden and hindrance to the gospel.

When it became apparent that such an important issue could not be settled in Antioch and that the debate had broad implications for the church, Paul, Barnabas, and some others were sent to Jerusalem to take the case to the elders and apostles there. When Paul and Barnabas arrived in Jerusalem, the leaders there welcomed them. The language implies they welcomed their affirmation of the Gentiles as well. However, once again, not everyone was pleased to hear about how the gospel had come to the Gentiles. The early church stood at the crossroads of what gospel it would preach to the world.

What are some beliefs and traditions we can hold on to that may impede the gospel for others?

The early church was proactive in dealing with a potential threat to the church's unity and mission. What lessons can we draw from their example?

Personal Study 2

The Discussion: Tradition vs. Scripture and Experience

Read Acts 15:6-18.

The church leaders gathered to consider the issue in what has been called the Jerusalem Council. Settling the issue at stake was critically important, but so was how the church would resolve it. To what would the church appeal to answer this question? Tradition or God's Word and what they had seen God do around them?

The issue was debated for some time, and then Peter stood to address the gathering and offered a strong defense of the Gentiles being saved by grace alone apart from circumcision. Peter reminded the gathering of his experience with Cornelius and how God had revealed Peter's need to cast aside a mind-set fixed on tradition and replace it with one fixed on the gospel (Acts 10–11). Circumcision had been a mark of purity and separateness from the world for God's people, but now in Christ, that mark comes by faith. In Christ, purity and separateness do not lead to salvation but instead flow out of it. Requiring circumcision before salvation undermined this essential aspect of the gospel.

Peter then appealed to God's giving of the Holy Spirit to the Gentiles as evidence of the Gentiles' conversion apart from circumcision. God had given the Gentile believers the Holy Spirit just as He had given the Holy Spirit to them. No distinction was made based on circumcision or any other factor—everyone had been saved by faith, and the giving of the Holy Spirit confirmed that God accepted that faith.

Peter concluded by asking why some were putting a yoke on the Gentile Christians' necks that neither their Jewish ancestors nor they could bear. They had appealed to God's grace for salvation, and so could the Gentiles.

To offer some background on the metaphor, the yoke was an agricultural implement carried by two oxen that allowed for straps to be attached so that a heavy plow could be moved forward. Jesus rebuked the Pharisees for the burdensome yoke they placed on people with their excessive teaching (Matt. 23:1-4). Peter was warning the early church not to do the same. Adding anything to faith alone for salvation was adding a heavy, unbearable yoke on their shoulders.

After Peter finished, the entire assembly, which just moments before had been in much debate, fell completely silent. Peter's strong defense of the gospel had resonated with the gathering. Paul and Barnabas then took the opportunity to echo Peter and share how they had experienced God work through them to see Gentiles come to faith. Paul and Barnabas relayed story after story of how God had transformed Gentile life after Gentile life.

Then it was James' turn. He began by affirming Peter's testimony, but then he pointed the gathering of Christians to the Scriptures. James quoted Amos 9:11-12 to show that what they had experienced recently with Gentiles coming to faith was part of God's plan all along. God had foretold their ancestors that everyone—Jews and Gentiles alike—would seek the Lord. The message of salvation had never been only for the Jews.

James concluded that based on what they had experienced and what God had revealed to them in Scripture, the church should not make it difficult for Gentiles to come to faith in Christ, which requiring circumcision would do. However, James also understood that there were ways that Gentile believers could threaten unity with the Jewish believers and also become a barrier to other Jews coming to faith in Christ. James suggested that the church write the Gentile believers and share what they could do to preserve the unity of the church.

What traditions have you had to set aside for the gospel?
How were you able to do so?

What are some of the dangers of relying only on our experiences to validate what God is doing?

Personal Study 3

The Decision: Freedom and Love

Read Acts 15:19-21.

The council of elders and apostles followed James' leadership and wrote a letter to be delivered to the Gentile believers in Antioch. Two men were selected to accompany Paul and Barnabas so there would be no questioning of the council's decision.

The letter began with a rebuke of the men who had come before raising the issue about circumcision. It was clear from the greeting that the church's ruling was in favor of the Gentile believers and that they were considered brothers and sisters in Christ.

All of the leaders in Jerusalem were concerned about the trouble the situation had caused the Gentile believers and they wanted to set the record straight. The leaders then made it clear that the decision they were sharing came through the Holy Spirit's wisdom and guidance and that no burdens should be placed upon them except for four requirements.

First, the Gentile believers were not to eat food offered to idols. It was a common practice among the Roman Empire that once food was offered as a sacrifice to their gods, it would then be prepared and shared in the pagan temple and even sold in the public market.

Second, the Gentile believers were not to eat food with blood still in it or used as an ingredient. Some Roman and Greek foods used blood as an ingredient, but Levitical law prohibited consuming blood. These foods might be offered at a wedding or a funeral feast, at a city festival, or even in common meals, but Gentile believers should now abstain from them.

Third, the Gentile believers were not to eat anything that had been strangled. Animals that were strangled instead of slaughtered retained the blood in them and could lead to it being consumed.

Fourth, the Gentile believers were to abstain from sexual immorality. The Greek word used here is the word from which we get the English word *pornography*. The Gentiles were known for engaging in loose and open sexual practices, both in daily relationships as well as in pagan worship. The church leaders probably assumed the Gentile believers would know to abstain from sexual fornication as part of worship practices. However, they might not have a clear understanding on the broader idea of sexual purity. Sexual encounters were of utmost intimacy and should be practiced only within committed marriage relationships.

This raises the question: "Why were these four practices singled out?"

James and the other leaders were concerned that the Gentile believers might take their personal freedom in Christ too far and live in such a way as to be a stumbling block to the convictions of their Jewish brothers and sisters. These four practices were addressed in Leviticus 17–18, where they were forbidden for both Jews and Gentiles living among the people of God. That is most likely why James mentioned that the Law of Moses was read every week in every synagogue in verse 21. These four prohibitions should not have surprised the Gentiles and they were of deep significance to the Jewish believers. If the Gentile believers abstained from these four practices, they would safeguard themselves from being a burden to the Jewish believers, ensure healthy fellowship between Jewish and Gentile Christ-followers, and not put a burden on other Jews coming to faith in Christ.

There is freedom in the gospel of Jesus Christ, but that freedom does not grant us the ability to do whatever we like. Freedom in Christ drives us back to God's love and kindness to us and compels us to extend love and kindness to others. Freedom and love go hand in hand.

What are some cultural practices today that are opposed to the gospel that we may need to clarify with new believers?

What freedoms have you given up, or should you give up, out of love for others?

The King Returns

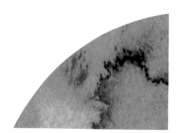
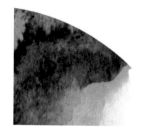
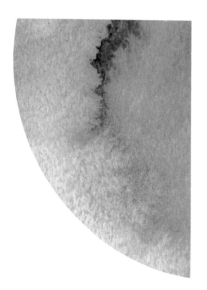

Introducing the Study

The Jerusalem Council was about more than settling a dispute over new believers. The very heart of the gospel was at stake: What was required for someone to be a true believer in Jesus Christ? Based on their knowledge of Scripture and the evidence of the Holy Spirit in the lives of Gentiles, they concluded that faith alone in Christ alone was the core of the gospel message—and the gospel went forth to the nations unhindered.

 Why do you think there is a tendency within us to add additional requirements to the gospel?

The expansion of the church was not without its challenges. At every turn, there was hostility and opposition to the gospel, and the believers often faced persecution. Still, the gospel spread as believers obeyed Jesus' Great Commission. Today, we continue in this mission. We continue living and proclaiming the truth of the gospel with hope, with confidence, that someday, perhaps today, Jesus will return. And we know that when He does, He will make all things new and we will live in an unhindered relationship with God forevermore.

How often do you think about the return of Christ? Why?

Setting the Context

In many ways, **the Book of Acts** reads like the commission from Jesus in Acts 1:8. The church started in Jerusalem, expanded to Judea, then crossed cultural boundaries into Samaria and eventually into the rest of the world. This spread of the gospel centered in large part on the missionary efforts of **the apostle Paul** as he traveled and planted churches in many cities, such as Ephesus, Philippi, and Corinth. Much of the remainder of the New Testament includes **the letters** of Paul, Peter, and others to the young churches and Christians across the land. These letters clarified points of doctrine and addressed specific problems that had arisen in their congregations and lives.

> Why is it that we can learn and grow from reading letters in the Bible written to churches and individuals?

The apostle John became a great apologist for the church, writing and preaching about the identity of Jesus, for which he was persecuted. As an old man he was exiled to the island of Patmos, where he received the vision we know as **the Book of Revelation**. God showed John a heavenly perspective on how God's story of redemption on earth would eventually come to an end with the return of Jesus Christ as the King of the universe, recognized by people from every tribe, language, people, and nation—the goal of **"The Gospel Mission"** (p. 83). When **Jesus returns**, He will make all things new, and with this new "In the beginning..." all of God's people will live forevermore in their resurrected bodies with our resurrected and reigning Savior.

 What are some benefits for the Christian who thinks regularly about the reality of Christ's return?

✝ CHRIST Connection

This present age will come to an end when Christ returns to fulfill His promises and reign with His people for all eternity. The relationship lost in the garden when Adam sinned will be gloriously restored when the garden city of the New Jerusalem is unveiled and Jesus wipes away every tear from every eye. The way to be part of God's new world is to be cleansed by the blood of the Lamb, shed for our redemption.

The **Gospel** *Mission*

GROUPS	OLD TESTAMENT	THE CHURCH	NEW CREATION
Tribe	The Twelve Tribes of Israel (Gen. 49:28; 2 Sam. 5:1)	James Wrote to "the Twelve Tribes" of Believers, Both Jew and Gentile (Jas. 1:1)	The Redeemed of God Through the Blood of the Lamb, Jesus Christ, Will Come from Every Tribe, Language, People, and Nation (Rev. 5:9-10; 7:1-17)
Language	Languages Confused at the Tower of Babylon (Gen. 11:7-9)	By the Spirit, the Disciples Preached the Gospel in Different Languages (Acts 2)	
People and Nation	The Different Family Lines and Kingdoms upon the Earth (Ps. 67)	A Holy Nation, a People for God's Possession (1 Pet. 2:9-10)	

"Jesus came near and said to them, 'All authority has been given to me in heaven and on earth. Go, therefore, and make disciples of all nations, baptizing them in the name of the Father and of the Son and of the Holy Spirit, teaching them to observe everything I have commanded you. And remember, I am with you always, to the end of the age.' " (Matt. 28:18-20)

Continuing the Discussion

 Watch this session's video, and then continue the group discussion using the following guide.

Why do you think so many people are fascinated by the Book of Revelation?

As a Christian, how should we read this book? Why do you think God included this revelation for us?

As a group, read Revelation 19:11-16.

 What names did John use to describe Jesus? What do these names for Jesus tell us about Him?

What do the descriptions of Jesus in this passage tell us about the results of His second coming?

The Rider's name is Faithful and True. Jesus never fails, and He is consistent in character. He comes to judge the earth precisely because He is faithful and true to God's will and His character. Furthermore, He is beyond our total understanding and is the ultimate Ruler. Together, these names tell us that Jesus is above all and that His majesty is beyond our comprehension.

As a group, read Revelation 21:1-5.

How would you summarize the message communicated by these images?

 Why is it significant that the Scripture emphasizes newness throughout this description of heaven?

The return of Jesus marks the newness of all things. Everything that came as a result of sin—pain, sickness, death, and sadness—will be undone. Christ will restore His creation to as good—or even better—than it had been originally. But most significant of all, the return of Jesus means that humanity will at last live in perfect communion with God. We will know Him as we are known by Him. We will no longer be separated in any way by the barrier of sin. This is the fulfillment of the gospel promise.

As a group, read Revelation 22:1-5.

 How do these images connect with the garden of Eden described in Genesis 2? What is the significance of those connections?

Based on what you've read in Revelation 21 and 22, what are some truths about heaven you can confidently declare?

Even after reading these passages of Scripture, we still can't point to many specific details about what heaven will be like. But we can look forward to some wonderful truths we do know about heaven. Through faith, we can stand firm on the belief that heaven is (and will always be) a place where we experience joy, peace, and love in the presence of Christ forever and ever. Amen.

✝ MISSIONAL Application

Record in this space at least one way you will apply the truth of Scripture as a sojourner in this land patiently longing with confidence and urgency for Jesus' return.

Personal Study 1

The conquering King will return to judge rebellion.

Read Revelation 19:11-16.

In the Old Testament, God ruled over the people as the King of Israel, but His reign was not sufficient in the hearts of the people. They wanted to be like the other nations (1 Sam. 8:5). God warned them that kings would oppress them and ultimately lead them astray, but they persisted in their demand. So God granted their request and raised up various kings to rule over the people.

One by one the kings failed. Even the faithful and good rulers such as David, Solomon, Hezekiah, and Josiah were frail and fallen leaders. But there was always a golden thread woven through the Old Testament pointing toward a coming King who would reign in perfect peace and righteousness (see Isa. 9:6-7; Jer. 23:5).

This king has come. He is Jesus the Christ, the Son of God. And He is coming again. This is good news, for the true King and the kingdom of righteousness will finally be consummated. Though Jesus secured His kingdom and lordship through His death and resurrection, His recognized reign will at last come to fruition upon His return. And with that will come the last judgment for rebellion against that kingdom.

The images in these verses are at the same time confidence-building and terrifying, for they are images of judgment. For the Christian, this should bolster our confidence. It reminds us that Jesus will not return as a baby, meek and mild, when very few recognized His true identity. That is how He came the first time, when He came as the Suffering Servant. But when Jesus returns, His identity will be clear, and all will see and recognize His power and glory. He is coming again as the conquering King. It is just a matter of time until He returns in full glory and power and makes all things right.

As Christians, then, we can live with confidence in the face of injustice and evil. When we bear witness to such things, it's easy for us to think that God is not paying attention or that the atrocities of men don't matter much to Him. After all, the righteous continue to suffer, and the unrighteous continue to prosper. We can very easily, like the psalmist, become frustrated and look to the sky crying, "Where are you God? Are you even noticing?"

But we should not mistake God's patience for His apathy. He sees. He knows. He cares. And when Jesus returns, He will bring justice and judgment with Him. In this we can have hope and confidence even while enduring wrongs and pain for the cause of Christ.

While the image of Christ returning in authority gives the Christian confidence, it brings terror to the rest of the world. There will come a day when it will be too late. Too late for repentance. Too late for belief. Too late to turn back. Justice will come.

In light of the sureness of God's judgment, we as Christians should confidently continue on in our gospel mission. We should share the gospel freely and liberally, without fear and with compassion for those not under God's grace, because the day is coming when King Jesus will judge.

How can you increase your confidence in the authority and power of Christ?

What are the implications of full confidence in the authority and power of Christ for how you live on mission for His kingdom?

Personal Study 2

The conquering King will return to make all things new.

Read Revelation 21:1-5.

In the vision God gave to the apostle John, He promised to make all things new. After the destruction of Satan, God will renew the created order of heaven and earth to make it a dwelling place for Himself and Christ's bride, the church. This echoes a prophecy given to Isaiah: God will create a new heaven and a new earth, and the former things shall not be remembered (Isa. 65:17).

Let's consider the characteristics of this new cosmos. We see a new city coming down from heaven from God. He is the One who has prepared and created this new city for Himself and His people.

The Book of Hebrews tells us that Abraham looked forward to a heavenly city whose builder and designer was God (Heb. 11:10). God told Abraham that He would make a people for Himself out of Abraham and that He would give them a land. The promised land that God swore to Abraham was a precursor to the better and heavenly one—a city that God has prepared for His people (v. 16). We have the hope that with the return of Christ, we will dwell as citizens in a "new Jerusalem."

In this vision, we also receive the wonderful promise of God's renewed presence with us for eternity. From start to finish, the Bible is the story of God's redemption of the world. When Adam and Eve sinned in Genesis 3, they were removed from the garden of Eden, out from the presence of God. But God made a promise to Abraham and his offspring: "I will be their God and they shall be My people." That promise is woven into the whole story of redemption (see Ex. 6:7; Lev. 26:12; Jer. 31:33; Ezek. 11:20).

God came to dwell with man in the most intimate of ways, by taking on human flesh (Matt. 1:23; cf. Isa. 7:14). As a result of Christ's work, God now dwells within every believer through His Holy Spirit (2 Cor. 6:16-18). And at the end of time, God will destroy all sin, renew the earth, raise up our bodies, and dwell with us fully and permanently in a renewed Eden (see Rev. 21:3).

To be in the presence of God for eternity is our greatest promise and hope. David's one desire was to dwell in the house of the Lord forever (Ps. 27:4). We see in David what man was originally created for—to know God intimately.

Additionally, Jesus said in John 17:3, "This is eternal life: that they may know you, the only true God, and the one you have sent—Jesus Christ."

The purpose for Christ's first coming was to make a way for us to be in God's presence. The purpose for His second coming is that we will be present with Him for eternity. If Jesus Himself is the greatest treasure in heaven, then He must be our greatest treasure on earth.

Finally, we see that the new cosmic order will be markedly different than the old one. The old creation was infected by evil and sin, in bondage to corruption (Rom. 8:21). This first creation will melt away and give way to a new heavens and earth in which righteousness dwells (2 Pet. 3:12-13).

For those who belong to Christ, this eternal home will be a place where death and grief no longer exist. The curse of death will be done away with forever because our perishable, mortal bodies will be renewed into imperishable, immortal bodies. Those who have put their faith in Christ in this world will be free to enjoy and cherish Him for eternity.

How have you traditionally viewed heaven? What are some popular misconceptions about heaven?

Do you long to be in the presence of God each day? Why or why not? What are some changes you can make to ensure you spend time with Jesus?

Personal Study 3

The conquering King will return to be with His people forever.

Read Revelation 22:1-5.

What will it be like? What will we experience when the conquering King returns? Revelation 22 gives us the briefest of glimpses, and it is glorious. What we find is a new Eden, one that has remnants of the first garden except this time in a city.

In his vision, the nearer John came to the center of the city, the more like a garden it became. It was like the garden of Eden, only better. A river watered Eden to provide life, and now a river gushed from the throne. As in the garden of Eden the tree of life is in the city. This tree of life mysteriously disappeared after being present in the first human home, but it reappears in the final human home wonderfully producing its fruit every month, unlike any tree now known. The tree's abundant harvest, as well as the healing effect of the leaves of the tree, show that heaven is filled with everything life-giving and glorious. Everyone there is healthy all the time.

Here, in this city, there is no curse. The curse of sin that came about in the first garden has, right now, infiltrated into every part of our human existence. Our relationships, our priorities, our emotions are all tainted by sin. But someday the curse will be no more. With this curse lifted, there will be only blessing. And that's when we get to the best part about this future: the throne of God and of the Lamb is there.

God's desire has always been to live in intimacy with His people. That they may know Him, even as He knows them. That they are fully and completely given over to being His people, for He is their God. This is our future.

Imagine that. In the future, we will no longer be torn in two different directions by the pull of sin and the pull of holiness. We will no longer have our minds wander when we try to focus on the greatness of God. We will no longer feel the temptation of sin and the sorrow that comes after. We will no longer live by faith because we won't need to any more. We will see the face of Jesus, and we will know Him.

This is truly what makes heaven, heaven. Yes, there are other glorious parts. There will be no more sickness. No more cancer. No more allergies. No more funerals. There will be no more injustice. No more retribution. No more societal struggles. But all of these things flow from the greatest thing of all—unbroken fellowship with God. This is what the entire Christian life points toward. And it's even bigger than that—this is what the entire story of redemption points toward. God is moving us, as His people, to the moment when we can truly and freely be with Him forever.

It's coming. We do not know when, but we know it will happen. In light of this, the end of the story—the beginning of eternity—should motivate us to live with urgency. We should unleash the message of the gospel and the work of the kingdom in every way we can, joining God in His mission to restore what has been broken by sin.

As we do so, we would do well to remember that the future is not in doubt. As John recorded the words of Jesus, "These words are faithful and true" (22:6).

Amen! Come, Lord Jesus!

Why do you think it's so important for Christians to have a vision of the future?

What are some specific ways you can pursue this vision of heaven even while you are on earth this week?

Tips for Leading a Small Group

Follow these guidelines to prepare for each group session.

Prayerfully Prepare

Review
Review the weekly material and group questions ahead of time.

Pray
Be intentional about praying for each person in the group. Ask the Holy Spirit to work through you and the group discussion as you point to Jesus each week through God's Word.

Minimize Distractions

Create a comfortable environment. If group members are uncomfortable, they'll be distracted and therefore not engaged in the group experience. Plan ahead by considering these details:

Seating

Temperature

Lighting

Food or Drink

Surrounding Noise

General Cleanliness

At best, thoughtfulness and hospitality show guests and group members they're welcome and valued in whatever environment you choose to gather. At worst, people may never notice your effort, but they're also not distracted. Do everything in your ability to help people focus on what's most important: connecting with God, with the Bible, and with one another.

Include Others

Your goal is to foster a community in which people are welcome just as they are but encouraged to grow spiritually. Always be aware of opportunities to include any people who visit the group and to invite new people to join your group. An inexpensive way to make first-time guests feel welcome or to invite someone to get involved is to give them their own copies of this Bible study book.

Encourage Discussion

A good small-group experience has the following characteristics.

Everyone Participates
Encourage everyone to ask questions, share responses, or read aloud.

No One Dominates—Not Even the Leader
Be sure that your time speaking as a leader takes up less than half of your time together as a group. Politely guide discussion if anyone dominates.

Nobody Is Rushed Through Questions
Don't feel that a moment of silence is a bad thing. People often need time to think about their responses to questions they've just heard or to gain courage to share what God is stirring in their hearts.

Input Is Affirmed and Followed Up
Make sure you point out something true or helpful in a response. Don't just move on. Build community with follow-up questions, asking how other people have experienced similar things or how a truth has shaped their understanding of God and the Scripture you're studying. People are less likely to speak up if they fear that you don't actually want to hear their answers or that you're looking for only a certain answer.

God and His Word Are Central
Opinions and experiences can be helpful, but God has given us the truth. Trust God's Word to be the authority and God's Spirit to work in people's lives. You can't change anyone, but God can. Continually point people to the Word and to active steps of faith.

How to Use the Leader Guide

Prepare to Lead

Each session of the Leader Guide is designed to be **torn out** so you, the leader, can have this front-and-back page with you as you lead your group through the session.

Watch the session teaching video and **read through the session content** with the Leader Guide tear-out in hand and notice how it supplements each section of the study.

Use the **Session Objective** in the Leader Guide to help focus your preparation and leadership in the group session.

Questions and Answers

✳ Questions in the session content with **this icon** have some sample answers provided in the Leader Guide, if needed, to help you jump-start the conversation or steer the conversation.

Setting the Context

This section of the session always has an **infographic** on the opposite page. The Leader Guide provides an activity to help your group members interact with the content communicated through the infographic.

MISSIONAL Application

The Leader Guide provides a **MISSIONAL Application statement** about how Christians should respond to the truth of God's Word. Read this statement to the group and then direct them to record in the blank space provided in their book at least one way they will respond on a personal level, remembering that all of Scripture points to the gospel of Jesus Christ.

Pray

Conclude each group session with a prayer. **A brief sample prayer** is provided at the end of each Leader Guide tear-out.

Session 1 · Leader Guide

Session Objective

Show how the Holy Spirit was given to fulfill the Father and Jesus' promise and to empower the church to live for Christ and complete the mission He gave.

Introducing the Study

Use these answers as needed for the question highlighted in this section.

- Earthly success, whether in our job or finances.
- Stability and permanency in where and how we live.
- The desire to please others, or even ourselves.

Setting the Context

Use these answers as needed for the question highlighted in this section.

- It was God's plan for the Holy Spirit to come at Pentecost, not at the ascension.
- To instill in the disciples the mind-set of waiting on God to move and lead, just as He had with the Israelites in the wilderness.
- So it was clear to them that God's wisdom and power in the Holy Spirit would help them fulfill the gospel mission, not their own wisdom or power.

Use the following activity to help group members see the blessing and assurance that come with the presence of the Holy Spirit.

Direct group members to look over the connections on **"Hearing the Old Testament in Acts"** (p. 11). Ask them to identify how these connections relate to the stories and promises of the Bible that have been covered in this study already. Then ask: "How are you encouraged by the fact that God's plan foretold in the Old Testament included the coming of the Holy Spirit and the existence of the church, of which you are a part as a believer in Christ?"

Read this paragraph to transition to the next part of the study.

Just as Jesus' crucifixion and resurrection were not God's Plan B, neither are the coming of the Holy Spirit and the church, with all her variety of people and gifts. God's Plan A, from before time and foretold in the Old Testament, includes us as believers in Christ, filled with the Spirit, gathered with the church, and living on mission for Jesus' name.

Continuing the Discussion

Watch this session's video, and then as part of the group discussion, use these answers as needed for the questions highlighted in this section.

Acts 2:1-4

- The power of the Holy Spirit is illustrated by the elements of wind and fire, both of which have the power to move and reshape God's creation.
- The purpose of the Holy Spirit is to come upon believers individually in Jesus Christ to empower them for the mission and to assure them of Christ's presence.
- The Holy Spirit empowers believers for communicating the gospel.

Acts 2:22-24,36-40

- The gospel must be heard so people can believe, but if there is no repentance and faith in response to the gospel, then people remain dead in their sins.
- Conviction of sin does not equate to knowing how to respond in faith, so sharing the gospel should involve a clear statement of response.
- Peter's instruction to the crowd helps us know how to respond to the gospel and how to lead others to respond to the gospel.

Acts 2:41-47

- The work of God in the salvation of sinners is a wonder to behold.
- The "fear of the LORD" refers to a deep reverence for our Creator and Savior; we dare not come to Him lightly, but we can come to Him in confidence.
- The fear of the Lord should lead to faith-filled obedience, acknowledging God's holiness and justice and rejoicing in His love, mercy, and grace.

Share the following statement with the group. Then direct them to record in the space provided in their book at least one way they will apply the truth of Scripture as a believer indwelt by the Holy Spirit and empowered for the gospel mission.

✝ MISSIONAL Application

Because we have been given the Holy Spirit and have been changed by Him, we fully rely on Him as we share the gospel, call people to repentance and faith, and live in community.

Close your group in prayer, thanking God for the gift of the Holy Spirit and asking Him to motivate you to give yourself fully to His mission.

Session 2 · Leader Guide

Session Objective

Show that persecution of the early church began from within Israel, resulting in the spread of the gospel and the strengthening of the church.

Introducing the Study

Use these answers as needed for the question highlighted in this section.

- Devotion to God's Word and to prayer.
- Devotion to love and fellowship with one another in the name of Jesus.
- The presence and power of the Holy Spirit.

Setting the Context

Use these answers as needed for the question highlighted in this section.

- Jesus suffered for us, so the suffering of Christians provides an opportunity to model Him in His suffering before a watching world.
- Most people run from suffering, but if Christians persist in the gospel mission even when persecuted, it bears witness to the worth of Christ.
- Faithful suffering shouts to the world that there is more to this life than what can be found and experienced in this world.

Use the following activity to help group members see the power of faithful suffering for the name of Jesus.

Instruct your group to look at **"Suffering for Jesus"** (p. 23). Ask them to point out any parallels they see between the suffering in the early church and the suffering Jesus experienced *(arrested, prayer, healings, tried and flogged by the Sanhedrin, continued faithfulness, wonders and signs, false accusations, death outside the city, prayer for forgiveness)*. Then ask the following questions: "Why do you think there are so many parallels in the suffering between the early church and Jesus?" "How is it possible to rejoice for being counted worthy to suffer for Jesus' name?" "What must the early church have believed about God the Father, God the Son, and God the Holy Spirit to have endured and rejoiced in suffering for Jesus' name?"

Continuing the Discussion

Watch this session's video, and then as part of the group discussion, use these answers as needed for the questions highlighted in this section.

Acts 6:8-10

- He was filled with the Holy Spirit.
- He was full of grace and power by the Spirit, performing miracles among the people.
- He spoke with wisdom and truth by the Spirit as he debated with those who opposed him.

Acts 7:44-51

- Stephen believed Scripture was true and trustworthy.
- Stephen believed the stories of Scripture had meaning and purpose that could be applied to life.
- Stephen believed the Scriptures work to convict the human heart of sin.

Acts 7:54-60

- Stephen's vision of Jesus standing in heaven affirmed the quality of his testimony to the gospel of Jesus.
- Jesus is typically referred to as seated in heaven, ruling over creation, so His standing shows great honor for Stephen.
- Jesus takes interest in the lives of His witnesses, and this vision is a reminder that Jesus is indeed with them to the end of the age.

Share the following statement with the group. Then direct them to record in the space provided in their book at least one way they will apply the truth of Scripture as a witness to the truth, grace, and glory of Jesus.

✝ MISSIONAL Application

Because Jesus suffered and died on our behalf, we bear witness to His greatness at all times, even when we are maligned or persecuted for the faith.

Close your group in prayer, praying that you would have the courage and conviction to stand for the gospel even if it is costly.

Session 3 · Leader Guide

Session Objective

Show how Philip was used to move the gospel outside of Jerusalem to Samaria and to a Gentile according to what Jesus had said in Acts 1:8. In a way, this session will lay the groundwork for the next few.

Introducing the Study

Use these answers as needed for the question highlighted in this section.

- The Holy Spirit convicts people of their sin so they recognize their need for the Savior.
- People may experience a life crisis that softens their heart to the gospel.
- God may have led an unbeliever to a verse or passage of Scripture that a Christian can explain and point to Jesus.

Setting the Context

Use these answers as needed for the question highlighted in this section.

- Pride and prejudice.
- Our own comfort and ease.
- Unbelief that certain people groups and nations are beyond the saving reach of God.

Use the following activity to help group members see how the gospel spread just as Jesus said it would.

Point out on **"Expansion of the Early Church in Palestine"** (p. 35) that Jesus' disciples were to begin their mission in Jerusalem and spread out to Judea and Samaria. Remind the group once again that persecution was the catalyst for the disciples leaving Jerusalem to fulfill this next step of the mission. Then ask the following questions:

- What are some ways the ministry of the disciples echoes that of Jesus? *(Philip preached in Samaria like Jesus; Peter healed a paralytic like Jesus; Stephen died outside Jerusalem like Jesus; Peter raised a little girl to life like Jesus.)*

- What are some similarities and differences between the mission efforts on this map and Joshua's mission of conquering the promised land? *(Both the disciples and Joshua and the Israelites traveled north and south to fulfill their missions; Joshua was sent in to destroy people and drive them out on account of their sin, but the disciples were sent to share the message of Jesus in order to save people from their sin; both Joshua and the disciples experienced miraculous orders and success.)*

Continuing the Discussion

Watch this session's video, and then as part of the group discussion, use these answers as needed for the questions highlighted in this section.

Acts 8:26-29

- Philip was quick to obey, even with vague and open-ended instructions.
- Philip was bold to approach someone whom he had never met.
- Philip was filled with the Holy Spirit, humble, and passionate about sharing the gospel.

Acts 8:30-35

- Be obedient, even when God's instructions take you outside of your comfort zone.
- Devote yourself to the apostles' teaching—God's Word—so you can answer questions from unbelievers with both knowledge and faith.
- Trust the Holy Spirit for direction and words when sharing the gospel with an unbeliever.

Acts 8:36-40

- That he believed the message about Jesus.
- That he wanted to respond with an act of obedience—baptism.
- The heart of a believer wants to obey the commands of Jesus.

Share the following statement with the group. Then direct them to record in the space provided in their book at least one way they will apply the truth of Scripture as a recipient of God's grace communicated through His Word about Christ.

MISSIONAL Application

Because Christ has revealed Himself to us through all of the Scriptures, we seek to be available and obedient to the Spirit's prompting, able and willing to share the Bible's story of salvation through Jesus.

Close your group in prayer, praying that you and your group would be obedient to the leading of the Holy Spirit for opportunities to share the gospel.

Session 4 · Leader Guide

Session Objective

Show how God was at work to save even the most unlikely of people in Saul and how he was given the task of advancing the gospel to the Gentiles. This connects back to the previous session, where we saw Philip share with one Gentile, and with the next session, where we see Saul and Barnabas sent on mission.

Introducing the Study

Use these answers as needed for the question highlighted in this section.

- We can see our suffering as serving a good purpose in the hands of God.
- Our suffering might serve as a witness to an unbeliever of the worth of Jesus in our lives.
- We can endure suffering knowing it will produce endurance in us and prepare us for even greater steps of faithfulness.

Setting the Context

Use these answers as needed for the question highlighted in this section.

- In one sense, the law emphasized the purity of the community of God, so unclean, uncircumcised Gentiles would have been shunned, and so were unclean and sinful Israelites; this was so the Israelites could be a pure light to the nations of God's glory.
- From the beginning, God's heart has been for the nations, that all people everywhere would be saved and welcomed into the people of God; God gives favor and blessing to His people, but He does not show favoritism to anyone.

Use the following activity to help group members see the power of God in a life changed by encountering Jesus.

Direct your group to review the timeline of **"Paul's Life"** (p. 47). Explain that Paul saw himself as an example of the extreme reach of God's patience and grace—if God could save him, He can save anyone (1 Tim. 1:12-17). Then ask the following questions:

- In what sense are we all like Paul, the worst of sinners (1 Tim. 1:15)? *(We all stand condemned before God on account of our sin, from the persecutor to the people-pleaser.)*

- What is the only difference between Paul "the Christian" and Paul "the Missionary"? *(Paul and Barnabas were set apart by the Holy Spirit for their missionary calling; otherwise, Paul was preaching and teaching everywhere he was, whether in his local context or on the mission field.)*

Continuing the Discussion

Watch this session's video, and then as part of the group discussion, use these answers as needed for the questions highlighted in this section.

Acts 9:3-9

- That Saul had been blind to the true nature and heart of God.
- That true sight comes from faith in Jesus, experienced in the community of the church.
- That truly Jesus is the One who gives sight to the blind.

Acts 9:10-16

- God has the power to change anyone's heart, even an enemy of the faith.
- God has His plans and purposes for people before they even come to faith in Jesus.
- Everyone God saves has the purpose of being a witness for Jesus wherever they are.

Acts 9:17-20

- Saul was no longer an enemy of God but a member of God's family in Christ.
- Saul was no longer a persecutor of the church but a brother in the faith with those whom he had come to imprison.
- Though temporarily blinded by the experience with Jesus, Saul was now a believer with a changed heart, mind, associations, and purpose.

Share the following statement with the group. Then direct them to record in the space provided in their book at least one way they will apply the truth of Scripture as one whose hardened heart has been changed by Jesus.

✝ MISSIONAL Application

Because we have been transformed by Christ in our salvation, we pray with full confidence that God can transform even the hardest heart.

Close your group in prayer, praying that you would be confident in the power of the gospel and be motivated to share boldly the good news of Jesus with the world.

Session 5 · Leader Guide

Session Objective

Show how God's chosen method of taking the gospel to all the world is missionaries, while also emphasizing that we are all to live on mission in our context.

Introducing the Study

Use these answers as needed for the question highlighted in this section.

- So we live with humility, knowing that our transformation from hardened sinners to children of God comes by the work of the gospel and the Holy Spirit.
- So we maintain our focus on spreading the gospel message and not a message of our own invention to tickle people's ears.
- So we evangelize with hope, knowing God can change anyone's heart.

Setting the Context

Use these answers as needed for the question highlighted in this section.

- Missionaries are supported by the church, but the prophets often ministered while being rejected by the people.
- Missionaries are sent to the nations; the prophets spoke messages against the nations and were only rarely sent to them.
- Prophets most often carried messages of judgment; missionaries carry the good news of the gospel of Jesus Christ.

Use the following activity to help group members see the strength and boldness that are available through the Holy Spirit in the lives of believers.

Draw attention to the map **"The First Missionary Journey of Paul"** (p. 59). Ask the group to describe the theme for Paul's stops on the mainland *(opposition; dangerous)*. Then ask the following questions: "Why do you think Paul and Barnabas faced such opposition in these cities?" "What temptations might they have faced in light of the opposition and danger for preaching the gospel?" "What can we know about their faith given that they retraced their steps through those same cities before returning home?"

Read this paragraph to transition to the next part of the study.

Surely Paul and Barnabas considered giving up and going home, or maybe they thought to dial down the intensity of the gospel message. But they did neither. They remained faithful to go where God led them and to say what God wanted them to say. They remained faithful, and that was good and right.

Continuing the Discussion

Watch this session's video, and then as part of the group discussion, use these answers as needed for the questions highlighted in this section.

Acts 13:1-3

- To be a church for all the nations.
- To be a church focused on and devoted to God and His will.
- To be a church that lived by faith.

Acts 13:4-8

- First to the Jew, then to the Gentile.
- They shared the gospel like scattering seed; they proclaimed the message about Jesus and then moved on to another town.
- They shared the gospel in public settings and by request with individuals.

Acts 13:9-12

- The miracle of judgment served to back up the missionaries' gospel message.
- Elymas's blindness demonstrated that his brand of religion as a Jewish false prophet was also blind, like Paul's experience after his encounter with Jesus.
- This miracle showed the Gentile proconsul that the missionaries worshiped the one true God, and he believed.

Share the following statement with the group. Then direct them to record in the space provided in their book at least one way they will apply the truth of Scripture as one who has benefited from the missionary efforts of Jesus' disciples.

✝ MISSIONAL Application

Because we are the beneficiaries of missionaries who went to the ends of the earth, we likewise consider becoming missionaries and we send and support others to go to those who have never heard the gospel.

Close your group in prayer, praying that you and your church would prioritize the mission of God appropriately.

Session 6 · Leader Guide

Session Objective

Show how the early church settled a vital dispute over the nature of salvation, which protected the gospel message that continued to be carried forth and also established a pattern of how the church is to settle disputes. This session needs to have a broad view of the rest of the church age, perhaps covering in the conclusion how the early church continued to carry this gospel message forward on two more missionary journeys by Paul and that it continues to hold the church together today.

Introducing the Study

Use these answers as needed for the question highlighted in this section.

- We should pray for God to raise up missionaries from within churches to go and make disciples of the nations.
- We should pray for the heart and the means to support missionaries as they go.
- We should pray to be sensitive to the leading of the Holy Spirit.

Setting the Context

Use these answers as needed for the question highlighted in this section.

- The requirement of circumcision was not isolated; it carried with it the expectation of full obedience to the law of Moses.
- Requiring circumcision for salvation didn't match up with the great success Paul and Barnabas had seen on their missionary journey.
- Requiring circumcision meant there could be a rift in the church between Jews and Gentiles, separating what God was bringing together.

Use the following activity to help group members see the importance of understanding the storyline of the Bible.

Ask your group to look at **"The Big Picture"** (p. 71). Explain that this summarizes the storyline of the Bible we have been studying. Allow your group members a couple of moments to comment on these headings, sharing details of the Bible stories they remember, explaining how the phases relate to one another, etc. Then ask this question:

- How does the nature of the fall setup the requirements for redemption? *(The fall came as the result of a prideful heart that wanted to be like God, and this sinful nature has been passed on to us all. Sin is more than just an external act; it is the fruit of a sinful heart. So redemption cannot come from external acts but only from a heart change.)*

Continuing the Discussion

Watch this session's video, and then as part of the group discussion, use these answers as needed for the questions highlighted in this section.

Acts 15:1-5

- It was preserving the heritage of the Jews.
- It was the jealousy of the older brother from Jesus' parable; they were refusing to celebrate the simple repentance of Gentile converts.
- These Jewish teachers still believed they could find salvation through keeping the law.

Acts 15:6-18

- The Father and the Son freely give the gift of the Holy Spirit to all who believe in Jesus' name.
- If the Gentile believers received the Holy Spirit apart from taking on circumcision, then it must not be required for salvation.
- The Holy Spirit is the down payment, the proof of our salvation, not circumcision.

Acts 15:19-21

- The gospel witness could continue unhindered among the Gentiles.
- The Christians were to be Jesus' witnesses in the world, not witnesses for the law of Moses.
- The few expectations for the Gentiles were to enable the gospel to be shared without hindrance by Gentile believers with Jewish unbelievers.

Share the following statement with the group. Then direct them to record in the space provided in their book at least one way they will apply the truth of Scripture as a sinner saved by grace alone through faith alone in Christ alone.

✝ MISSIONAL Application

Because we recognize our desperate need of grace and the sufficiency of Christ in our lives, we proclaim a message that salvation is available through faith in Christ alone, and no additional obligations and works are necessary.

Close your group in prayer, thanking God for the simple truth of the gospel and praying that you would be able to keep that truth unpolluted.

Session 7 · Leader Guide

Session Objective

Show how the gospel story ends with Jesus' return and all things being made new, all of the consequences of sin being dealt with, and us enjoying eternal, unhindered relationship with God as He intended. We should stress that this is our hope and the fullness of the gospel—it does not end with our personal salvation; we are still growing in the gospel as we continue to look forward to this day.

Introducing the Study

Use these answers as needed for the question highlighted in this section.

- In our pride, we want to save ourselves.
- It feels too easy to say salvation is by faith alone in Christ.
- We want to compare ourselves to other people and measure them by our standards—again, pride.

Setting the Context

Use these answers as needed for the question highlighted in this section.

- Hope for endurance in the daily trials and struggles of this life.
- Encouragement to live faithfully, knowing the Savior is coming soon.
- An urgency to live on mission for the glory of Jesus' name among the nations.

Use the following activity to help group members see the purpose and the result of the gospel mission we have received.

Direct your group to read over **"The Gospel Mission"** (p. 83). Ask the group to identify ways the gospel mission of the church picks up on themes that have been communicated through the storyline of Scripture *(God's heart for the nations; reconciliation among the peoples; all praise and glory to the Son for His obedience to the cross and resurrection)*. Then ask the following questions: "How has the storyline of Scripture helped you to better understand the identity and work of Jesus?" "How have you been encouraged to live on mission in light of the Bible's storyline?"

Read this paragraph to transition to the next part of the study.

The storyline of Scripture helps to make sense of the various stories of the Bible, but even more so, it helps us see the importance of Jesus' coming and second coming and challenges us to obey Jesus and live on mission for the sake of His great name. Let us not miss the point of Scripture: Let us point everyone to Jesus just as the Bible does.

Continuing the Discussion

Watch this session's video, and then as part of the group discussion, use these answers as needed for the questions highlighted in this section.

Revelation 19:11-16

- *Faithful and True:* Jesus is trustworthy, faithful, and always keeps His promises.
- *The Word of God:* Jesus communicates and acts in complete alignment with God because He is God. His Word is powerful and never fails.
- *King of Kings and Lord of Lords:* Jesus' rule is supreme over all other kings, lords, rulers, and authorities. Everyone will bow to Him.

Revelation 21:1-5

- The current heavens and earth are marred by sin and awaiting redemption.
- The Christian looks forward to the second coming of Jesus in part because of the promise of the resurrection to new bodies free from sin and death.
- God has promised since the beginning that the serpent will be crushed by His Son, and this will entail a new start free from temptation and sin.

Revelation 22:1-5

- The tree of life is available to all believers in the new heavens and new earth, so eternal life is guaranteed.
- There will no longer be any curse; the work of human beings will again be joyful and completely God-glorifying as we obey God with our whole hearts.
- God's presence is once again with humanity in His fullness, unhindered by sin and never to be lost again.

Share the following statement with the group. Then direct them to record in the space provided in their book at least one way they will apply the truth of Scripture as a sojourner in this land patiently longing with confidence and urgency for Jesus' return.

✝ MISSIONAL Application

Because we carry the unwavering hope within us that Jesus will return at any time and make all things new, we live with confidence and joy and also urgency as we share the hope of the gospel with others.

Close your group in prayer, thanking God for the promise that He is in control of all history and is bringing it together under the lordship of Christ.

HE GAVE HIMSELF FOR US

to redeem us from
all lawlessness
and to cleanse for himself
a people for his own possession,
eager to do good works.

TITUS 2:14

FROM COVER
TO COVER,

the Bible is the story of God's plan to redeem sinners through Jesus—the gospel. Gospel Foundations tells that story.

———

Be sure to take advantage of the following resources if you're planning a churchwide study. Even the *Single Group Starter Pack* offers significant savings.

CHURCH LAUNCH KIT (DIGITAL)

Want to take your entire church through Gospel Foundations? You'll want a *Church Launch Kit*. It includes sermon outlines, promotional graphics, and a Wordsearch Bible digital library for all leaders valued at $330. The *Kit* comes complimentary with every *Church Starter Pack*. Also available separately.

$29.99

———

Order online, call 800.458.2772, or visit the LifeWay Christian Store serving you.

STARTER PACKS

You can save money and time by purchasing starter packs for your group or church. Every *Church Starter Pack* includes a digital *Church Launch Kit* and access to a digital version of the *Leader Kit* videos.

Single Group Starter Pack
(10 *Bible Study Books*, 1 *Leader Kit*)
$99.99

Church Starter Pack - Small
(50 *Bible Study Books*, 5 *Leader Kit* DVDs, *Church Launch Kit*)
$449.99

Church Starter Pack - Medium
(100 *Bible Study Books*, 10 *Leader Kit* DVDs, *Church Launch Kit*)
$799.99

Church Starter Pack - Large
(500 *Bible Study Books*, 50 *Leader Kit* DVDs, *Church Launch Kit*)
$3495.99

LifeWay.com/GospelFoundations

Prices and availability subject to change without notice.

Continue your study of the bigger story of Scripture—daily.

With The Gospel Project *Daily Discipleship Guide*, you'll find that the content will still immerse you in the storyline of Scripture with these significant benefits:

Combines the Group Experience with Daily Bible Study

You attend the group and then build upon what you learned using five daily devotionals.

Guest Friendly

Everyone who comes to the group starts on the same page. So guests, and even participants who've been absent for a while, won't feel like they've missed anything because they didn't study before the meeting.

Great for Discipleship Groups

Group members that meet in smaller groups for deeper discipleship will love the Encourage One Another section. This gives them more questions to discuss that week's study.

Enhanced Experience for Leaders

The *Leader Guide* is available separately and includes a group plan and commentary to help you guide your group through each session.

Download a free preview at GospelProject.com/Adults

Group Directory

Name: _____   Name: _____
Home Phone: _____   Home Phone: _____
Mobile Phone: _____   Mobile Phone: _____
Email: _____   Email: _____
Social Media: _____   Social Media: _____

Name: _____   Name: _____
Home Phone: _____   Home Phone: _____
Mobile Phone: _____   Mobile Phone: _____
Email: _____   Email: _____
Social Media: _____   Social Media: _____

Name: _____   Name: _____
Home Phone: _____   Home Phone: _____
Mobile Phone: _____   Mobile Phone: _____
Email: _____   Email: _____
Social Media: _____   Social Media: _____

Name: _____   Name: _____
Home Phone: _____   Home Phone: _____
Mobile Phone: _____   Mobile Phone: _____
Email: _____   Email: _____
Social Media: _____   Social Media: _____

Name: _____   Name: _____
Home Phone: _____   Home Phone: _____
Mobile Phone: _____   Mobile Phone: _____
Email: _____   Email: _____
Social Media: _____   Social Media: _____

Name: _____   Name: _____
Home Phone: _____   Home Phone: _____
Mobile Phone: _____   Mobile Phone: _____
Email: _____   Email: _____
Social Media: _____   Social Media: _____